Politics, Cultures and Communication

Published with the Aspen Institute for Humanistic Studies

Politics, Cultures and Communication

European vs. American
Approaches to
Communications Policymaking

ROLAND S. HOMET, JR.

PRAEGER PUBLISHERS

PRAEGER SPECIAL STUDIES

NEW YORK   LONDON   SYDNEY   TORONTO

Library of Congress Cataloging in Publication Data

Homet, Jr., Roland S   1932–
    Politics, cultures and communication.

    At head of title: Aspen Institute for Humanistic
Studies, Program on Communications and Society.
    Includes bibliographical references.
        1. Communication—Europe.   I. Aspen Institute
Program on Communications and Society.   II. Title.
P92.E9H65   301.16'1'094   79-9817
ISBN 0-03-049786-8

PRAEGER PUBLISHERS, PRAEGER SPECIAL STUDIES
383 Madison Avenue, New York, N.Y., 10017, U.S.A.

Published in the United States of America in 1979
by Praeger Publishers,
A Division of Holt, Rinehart and Winston, CBS Inc.
9 038 987654321
© 1979 by Aspen Institute for Humanistic Studies

Printed in the United States of America

Contents

Foreword

As an international institution seeking to stimulate interchange among societies and sectors of society worldwide, the Aspen Institute attempts to define and review the varying ways in which such groups meet common problems. Frequently, individual societies will evolve differing solutions even though the original public policy issue and even the technology involved may be identical or at least very similar. Cross-societal comparisons, which involve different sets of basic values and priorities, can be useful to those in each society who have to deal with ongoing problems.

This volume is an integral part of the Institute's continuing effort to participate constructively in the process by which societies learn from each other and affect one another's future.

Roland Homet's study is a product of the second phase of the Aspen Institute's Program on Communications and Society. The Program was directed for many years by Douglass Cater, and Michael Rice is now its Director. Mr. Homet served as the Program's Director before going to Europe to develop this survey. He is presently the Director of International Communications Policy of the International Communication Agency in Washington, D.C.

In its second phase, the Program on Communications and Society focused on such critical issues as government-media relations and policies and the better use of communications technology. The present volume should be viewed in relation to *Communications for Tomorrow—Policy Perspectives for the 1980s* edited by Glen O. Robinson, Special Adviser to the Aspen Institute and Professor of Law at the University of Virginia.

Both volumes result from the generous assistance of the Ford Foundation and the John and Mary R. Markle Foundation, which helped define the project and its key issues and identify many of the participants and provided the support that made the entire undertaking possible. The studies were also aided significantly by the Rockefeller Brothers Fund, the Charles F. Kettering Foundation and the Edna McConnell Clark Foundation.

Special notes of gratitude are owed to McGeorge Bundy, Fred Friendly and David Davis of the Ford Foundation and to Lloyd Morrisett and Jean Firstenberg of the Markle Foundation for their personal interest and contributions to the project. William Dietel and Robert Bates of the Rockefeller Brothers Fund, Robert Chollar and Kent Collins of the Kettering Foundation and Merrell Clark of the Clark Foundation gave substantially of their time and support.

The Institute's Program on Communications and Society, in its present third phase, emphasizes its concern about the emerging problem of communications policy in relation to the quality of contemporary life. The interrelationships between the worlds of education and communications are being given special attention as major forces in the emergence of the individual in the first 20 years of life, as well as in continuing education. The problems of stimulating creativity through diversity and the maintenance of standards of excellence and of sustaining the ability to remain lively and experimental are being approached as the sine qua non of the advancement of culture and human values.

By seeing how comparative societies are meeting—or failing to meet—the challenges presented by new communications needs and technology, the reader can better understand his own nation's approaches to upgrading media content and standards, creating access to the media by new talent from his country and abroad, the relationships between government and media, the social impact of the media and other policy issues of immediacy.

Mr. Homet's study covers six European countries that permit useful comparisons to approaches and practices in the United States. Although Canada and Japan are not included in this report, the Program on Communications and Society has held consultative conferences in both countries and a separate volume entitled *Japanese Public Broadcasting—A Promise Fulfilled* by Judith Geller was published by the Institute earlier this year.

Here, Mr. Homet observes that in Western Europe communications policy issues tend to be kept under political control rather than turned over to the open competition of the marketplace. He found benefits in this: order, stability, the avoidance of wasteful duplication of services and a concentration on engineering and cultural quality not subject to popular referendum. However, he also found that decisions are taken in the governmental ministries and state corporations that control telecommunications and broadcasting with virtually no participation by interested industries or members of the public. Although he did find a tradition for the support of significant work which requires time, money and freedom for the author to produce, control is concentrated in ever fewer hands. As a result, European broadcasting pays a price in diminished democratic participation and risks overlooking significant policy options. In addition, present governmental structures are often unable to accommodate to the rapid evolution in communications technologies and services.

Mr. Homet also concluded that the emphasis in the United States on freedom of the press and public access to means of communication does not have its counterpart in the European countries he investigated. Indeed, there is fear in some places that television, in particular, could usurp political functions of debate and conciliation and thereby reduce the role of political leaders. And finally, he suggests, the monopolistic structure of European communications tends to inhibit the flourishing of diverse and pluralistic talents. In most of Western Europe, formal and informal restraints limit the free expression of ideas over the airwaves. On the other hand, he found that public affairs analysis is frequently very good and that Eurovision has made contributions to the independence of a new generation in Europe.

Among the basic differences he discovered between the approaches in the United States and in Western Europe, commercial broadcasting dominates in the United States while in Europe it plays a secondary role behind government-controlled broadcasting. In addition, the regulatory commission, so familiar in the United States and Canada, does not exist in the countries studied.

At the heart of the intriguing and crucial issues and approaches discussed in this book are questions of values. These differ among cultures and are based on history that has left many key Europeans as suspicious of business dominance of communications as many Americans are distrustful of governmental controls.

In the absolutely crucial field of public communication, all of us can see clearly how varying approaches to the problems of governance affect our lives, our well-being and our future. Society has fewer more pressing issues before it in this era of dramatic technological change than how we shall organize the ways we communicate with each other and what we have to communicate.

Joseph E. Slater
President
Aspen Institute for Humanistic Studies

Origins and Acknowledgments

In 1976 the Aspen Institute for Humanistic Studies launched a major multi-year inquiry into the way that communications policy is perceived and dealt with at the official level in the United States. Given that scholars have detected a gathering communications "revolution," to quote John Adams' plaint in the musical comedy *1776:* "Is anybody listening? Does anybody care?" Those who did care enough to organize and lead an orchestrated inquiry include the President of the Aspen Institute, Joseph Slater, and the Institute's then Program Council Director, Douglass Cater, who together made the entire project possible; Shepard Stone, Director of the Aspen Institute Berlin, who hosted two conferences on the subject, with distinguished West European participation; and my colleagues in the Aspen Institute Program on Communications and Society: Glen Robinson, Henry Geller, Forrest Chisman and Marc Porat. My thanks go to each of them, to the distinguished scholars and policy analysts who joined us, and to the leaders of U.S. industry and labor and government and public-interest groups who consented to share their perceptions.

The present essay must be seen as a companion piece to the major report produced by that venture, entitled *Communications for Tomorrow: Policy Perspectives for the 1980s.* By design, that report concentrates on the situation in the United States. From the beginning, however, the importance of a comparative perspective has been recognized. Consultative conferences were held during March 1977 in Toronto, London and Berlin and a further conference for the same purpose was held in Tokyo in May 1978. It would obviously be desirable to commission monographs on comparative policymaking in Japan, Australia and Canada—all countries with advanced communications systems, opportunities and risks. A start had to be made somewhere, however, and the decision reached was to look first at Western Europe where similarities and differences with the American communications picture are sufficiently pronounced to foster useful comparisons.

This essay is the outgrowth of that decision. It is based to some extent on official and unofficial documents—particularly on the recent reports of four inquiry committees in Britain and West Germany—that are available to any interested reader. But it is dependent even more, for tone and nuance and context, on a series of conferences, conversations and meetings held in Western Europe in the autumn and winter of 1977–78.

Here too, choices have had to be made; and the reader will find an emphasis on the situations in Britain, France and West Germany, where the more detailed inquiries were conducted. Economically and culturally these are probably the most prominent of the West European societies, while the differences among them yield significant contrasts. But there is also much to be learned from the distinctive ways in which Italy, the Netherlands and Sweden have organized themselves to deal with communications and especially broadcasting; this essay looks at them as well.

It is difficult to single out the Europeans who have been most helpful in my researches, yet to list all those who have been willing to share their knowledge and perceptions would be too lengthy. I hope those not specifically mentioned will understand and accept a general reiteration of the gratitude I expressed at the time.

The International Institute of Communications in London, directed by Edward Ploman, was a thoughtful intellectual host throughout the study. Asa Briggs, the IIC trustee with principal responsibility for research, was unfailingly generous with his time and suggestions. Mrs. Joanna Spicer, the IIC's research director, opened her library and suggested people and shared relevant work-in-progress. Chairman Jean d'Arcy was extremely helpful in arranging an entire week's worth of interviews in Paris. John Howker offered continuously valuable indirect assistance through his editorship of the bimonthly IIC publication *Intermedia*, which, as a glance at the footnotes will show, provides a highly useful compendium of information and analysis on communications developments in Western Europe and around the world.

In greater London, thanks are due to Michael Tyler and his colleagues at Communications Studies and Planning Ltd., who gave many useful leads and also set aside office space for our use; Revel Guest, who shared her knowledge of the BBC and the special tribulations and triumphs of the independent producer in today's television environment; Colin Young, director of the National Film

School, who offered his perceptions of how talent fares in the film and television markets; Alex Reid and his associates in the Long Range Studies Division of British Post Office Telecommunications, who made available an inside view of policy analysis and planning and also explained the developmental plans for Viewdata; Lord Annan and Professor Hilde Himmelweit, both of whom came to the first Aspen Institute Berlin conference in March 1977 and then and later discussed the key points of controversy in the Annan Committee report on broadcasting; Charles Carter, the chairman of the Carter Committee on posts and telecommunications, who came to an IIC evening in London to explain and answer questions on his report; and Lord Harris of Greenwich, the minister responsible for broadcasting in the Home Office, who gave his political insights into the evolving relationship between government and the mass media.

Special recognition is owing to Anthony Smith, the author of several relevant works of which *The Shadow in the Cave: The Broadcaster, the Audience, and the State* (Quartet Books, 1976) provides a literate and perceptive context for the appreciation of differences between and among European and American broadcasting systems. Smith made a number of very useful comments; and, together with Michael Tyler, he read Part II (Institutional and Industry Structure) in draft and corrected factual misconceptions.

Smith also helped organize the second of two Aspen Institute Berlin conferences bearing on the subject matter of this project. (All those attending the two conferences are listed in the Appendix.) The authors of papers on television and politics at this second conference provided information and outlook that I found particularly helpful: Smith himself (Britain); Antoine de Tarlé (France); Professor Alfred Grosser (West Germany); Herman Wigbold (Netherlands); Åke Ortmark (Sweden); and Fabio Luca Cavazza (Italy)—who could not attend the conference but whose paper was highly stimulating. The papers when edited are to be published under the tentative title, *Politics in Camera: Television in the Political Life of Western Europe.*

Among the Germans at the second Berlin conference who contributed a great deal towards an understanding of broadcasting in West Germany were: Klaus von Bismarck, President of the Goethe Institute; Gerd Kopper, of the SPD Executive Committee; and Lothar Loewe and Dietrich Schwarzkopf from the broadcasting station Norddeutscher Rundfunk. Earlier, I twice had the benefit of extended discussion with Dr. Eberhard Witte, chairman of the

KtK commission on the future of German telecommunications. And I met in Berlin with Colin Young's opposite number in schooling for films and television: Dr. Heinz Rathsack, director of Deutsche Film und Fernschakademie.

Further guidance to the situation in Italy was supplied by Furio Colombo, foreign correspondent for *La Stampa,* who attended the first Berlin conference and gave a diverting account of Italian developments. Also in attendance on that occasion was Jean Voge, who directs training in both broadcasting and telecommunications for technicians and managers not just in France but in all of *francophonie;* his sense of technology thrust and of social implications has value for all societies facing the changes wrought by new communications systems.

In and around Paris, Jean d'Arcy arranged meetings with international and national bodies. I had earlier met and worked with Hans Peter Gassman, who was instrumental in setting up the OECD's subgroup on Information, Computers, and Communications Policy; he came to the first Aspen Institute Berlin conference and contributed his views. In January 1978 I met Asher Deleon, the staff director of the new UNESCO International Commission for the Study of Communication Problems, and also talked to several of his colleagues about how that body is or might become engaged in assessing the effects of new communications technologies and services.

On the French scene itself, I had meetings with a number of people at the Haut Conseil de l'Audiovisuel, the Institut National de l'Audiovisuel, the IDHEC film and television training school, and elsewhere. Jean d'Arcy's good friend Jean Diwo, editor of *Télé 7 Jours,* provided insight into French broadcasting as it is actually practiced. And I toured the National Assembly and the committee rooms with Antoine de Tarlé, which provided a further opportunity to develop the perceptions he had opened up in Berlin.

Naturally, none of these people is to be blamed for failures of understanding that may be displayed in this essay. I am grateful for their efforts to steer me along a path of enlightenment, but what I have done with their guidance is entirely my own responsibility.

Finally, my appreciation goes to Debra C. Hinck for her very helpful research assistance and for her patience in drawing what coherence there was to be found out of the successive drafts imposed on her.

The factual research for this essay was concluded in the spring of 1978. Subsequent developments are sure to have altered at least some of the events or conditions I describe—for example, the reception by the British Government of the inquiry-committee reports. My principal interest, however, lies in drawing the reader's attention to underlying trends and tendencies.

R.H.
Minster Lovell
U.K.

Guide to European Committees of Inquiry

Short name	Formal title
KtK	Commission for the Development of the Tele-communications System (West Germany)
Annan Committee	Committee on the Future of Broadcasting (U.K.)
Carter Committee	Post Office Review Committee (U.K.)
Royal Commission	Royal Commission on the Press (U.K.)

I
Introductory
Overview

1976–1978 provides a propitious period in which to undertake a comparative assessment of communications policies and policy-making in Western Europe. During this time, high-speed, low-cost and versatile new communications techniques—many of them directly competitive with the traditional services of broadcasting, telephony, the mails and the print press—began to make their presence felt in both Europe and the United States. The resulting challenge is not just to the continued vitality of established services on which people now depend for their information, entertainment and social and business discourse. It is also to the institutional structures by which these services are provided and to the regulatory or supervisory arrangements under which they operate. Forces of innovation and of conservation in communications sooner or later seek vindication in the policy arena, and the response of governments to their collision is indicative of the values attached to the function of information exchange in each society.

This clash of forces is at present a national and not an international issue. In 1977, UNESCO did establish a new International Commission for the Study of Communications Problems, but its chief preoccupation is with the specific and highly contentious issues of cross-boundary media content and control. About a year earlier, the OECD created a subgroup dealing with "Information, Computers, and Communications Policy," but to date it has served as a gathering place for experts and its work has had little policy recognition even in the United States, which plumped for its creation.

1

In particular, the concept of an "Information Society"—the creature of American scholars seeking to emphasize the dynamic importance of information transactions within the economically advanced societies—has had some acceptance within the OECD subgroup but has gained no currency whatever in official West European policy deliberations. This reflects, among other things, a present disinclination to be drawn into integrative or long-range communications policy formulation. West European governments are disposed to make up their own minds at their own speed about the place of communications in their own societies, and they are likely to proceed incrementally rather than by sudden adoption of any grand design.

That makes the study of the fledgling policy process all the more intriguing. In the 1976–1978 period, four full-scale reports were produced by independent committees of inquiry appointed by West European governments for this purpose. In West Germany, the Commission for the Development of the Telecommunications System (the KtK), under the chairmanship of Dr. Eberhard Witte, looked at the new electronic communications technologies and services and addressed the problem of integrating these developments into established patterns of industrial and government organization.[1] In Britain three separate reports were published in 1977. The Committee on the Future of Broadcasting, chaired by Lord Annan (the Annan Committee), examined possible arrangements for a fourth broadcasting channel, for newer technologies such as broadband cable and teletext, and for various institutional and procedural innovations.[2] The Post Office Review Committee, chaired by Mr. Charles Carter (the Carter Committee), dealt with both postal and telecommunications services and with the organizational structure for them.[3] And the Royal Commission on the Press, chaired by Professor, now Lord, McGregor (the Royal Commission) inquired into the economic health of a highly concentrated industry and into the advisability, among other things, of government subsidies and of a strengthened Press Council.[4]

Parochial considerations seem to have played a good part in creation of these inquiry committees. Governments felt the need to dampen enthusiasm for full-blown commercial or cable television, to justify extension of existing broadcast licenses, to downplay financial losses on conventional mail service, even to make a ritual expression of solicitude for the welfare of a largely opposition press. Once the four committees were established, however, the problems presented to them proved both larger and more complex than those motivating their appointment. As a result, the reports of the inquiry committees are a valuable source of information for comparative analysis. Among them they tend to show which issues of communications policies are given priority attention, what sets of values or governing considerations are applied to their resolution, and by what kinds of processes and institutions they are decided.

There is no single or uniform West European approach to communications policymaking. Significant differences exist between countries and among various classes of communications services. The press is unregulated, posts and telecommunications tightly controlled. Yet some governments favor press subsidies, while others at least formally shy away. Some governments foster technical and service innovation by their PTT's (post and telecommunications organizations), others struggle and hold back. There is wide divergence in the amount of freedom allowed to broadcasting entities and in the degree of pluralistic participation in broadcast programming. When it comes to admitting new services like broadband cable or teletext or packet switching, with the potential for undermining the economic viability of established services, inertial resistance is fairly uniform, but emphases differ considerably.

Generalizations are accordingly hazardous, which is not surprising when one considers that policymaking is an attribute of political culture and that cultures are formed by the whole history of a people. French policy perspectives have been shaped by a history very different from that informing Dutch perspectives, and British institutions have grown up under very different influences from those affecting Italian institutions. As we discover variations in approach among West European governments, we may also catch glimpses of underlying and persisting differences in political culture. We may even find occasions, like the French broadcasting reforms of 1974, when a change of institutional structure produces no real policy change because the culture has been unaffected.

But if there is no uniformity, there are common tendencies in West European policymaking, which can be made to stand in relief when they are contrasted to the ways that communications policy is decided in North America. The independent regulatory commission, enshrined in the communications landscape of America and

Canada, finds no counterpart in any West European country. Commercial broadcasting, the premier service in the United States, is given at best a secondary place in the broadcasting systems of Western Europe. The stress in American policy debates on the invigorating virtues of marketplace competition is given some lip service in Europe as regards the press, control over which is falling into ever fewer hands, but virtually no recognition in other sectors of communications policy.

Are these differences merely happenstance? It seems more likely that they are outgrowths of the dissension of the European settlers who populated North America—men and women seeking to escape from social rigidities, to exercise a larger measure of economic freedom, to form governments and government structures that they might control rather than the other way around. Of course, not all the American aspirations have been realized in the last 200 years, any more than European societies have stood still. Social democracy, for example, is a conception of 19th century Europe; today there are Social Democratic parties in power in West Germany and Britain (and, some say, eventually coming in France) but none in the United States. Yet actual policies are still formulated by people—who are products of their whole culture, its class structures, its historic attitudes towards public service and private freedom.

So an examination of comparative policymaking is likely to yield insights into the state of comparative political cultures today on the two sides of the North Atlantic. It should operate in both directions, making possible an evaluation of American institutions through European eyes no less than the reverse. This added dimension could be of some value to policy analysts accustomed to gauging public performance in their own societies by professions of purely domestic objective. How we are doing by others' lights, as well as by our own, is at any rate a question that comparative policy assessment should aim to open up.

It is customary to divide public communications enterprises into separate categories: electronic vs. print, mass media vs. point-to-point, distributed vs. switched. The print media are generally free from government control in Western societies, while electronic communications services are subject to varying degrees of government supervision. The point-to-point services, like telephony and the mails, are governed as common carriers having a duty to carry without discrimination any messages presented to them. The mass electronic media, on the other hand, are expected to choose messages for transmission (news, entertainment, information) exercising their own editorial judgments subject to certain standards imposed on them by governments. Switched services operate to link people (or computers) together individually, one-to-one, whereas distributed services like publishing or broadcasting emanate to an audience from a central point, one-to-many.

These categories have been generally accepted by both Western Europeans and North Americans for structural and policy purposes. Differing institutional and regulatory consequences have flowed from the placement of a service in one category or another. Today those categories are breaking down as a result of new and versatile communications and computing technologies whose service capacities overflow the conventional boundaries. But for comparative purposes it is still useful to start with the traditional set of shared assumptions.

Point-to-point services in Western Europe are organized into post and telecommunications administrations, under the form of nationalized monopoly industries or government departments. The British Post Office, an independent state corporation, looks rather like the U.S. Postal Service but does not at all resemble the Bell System. The division of authority between regulation and management in North America, where independent regulatory agencies oversee the telephone industry, is much more pronounced than is that between management and political supervision in Western Europe, where there are no such agencies.

The electronic mass medium of broadcasting is also organized as a state controlled monopoly or oligopoly in Western Europe but with structures affording greater independence from government. Yet there is no disposition to adopt the American model of broadcasting as a dominantly commercial enterprise exercising itself to maintain the maximum possible separation from government.

Perhaps the major distinction from U.S. practice is the steadfast resistance of all West European countries to commercial domination of their broadcasting systems. Brand advertising is permitted on at least some channels in virtually all these countries, but each has adopted measures designed to restrain competitive programming aimed at the lowest common denominator of mass audience tastes. This fear of commercial distortion is every bit as strong and pervasive as is, in the United States, the fear of government intervention.

The tradition of a free and independent print press, supported by advertising as well as circulation, is on the other hand observed with fair similarity on both sides of the North Atlantic. Subsidies to newspapers are rather more cheerfully dispensed and accepted in Western Europe, and the Press Councils operate as organs of industry self-regulation with much wider acceptance than their counterpart enjoys in the United States. But these differences between European and American practice, significant as they may be, are less important than the similarities. There are no government agencies with authority to supervise the output of the press, no requirement of "fairness" or balance in newspaper coverage. There are ritual expressions of concern about the growing concentration of ownership among newspapers, but just as in the United States very little is done about it.

Yet change is coming in both places, and newspapers may be among those leading the way. The high costs of labor and of newsprint are forcing a search for cost savings, which, with recent technological advances, may be found through such expediting techniques as electronic editing, computer adjustment and photocomposition. If labor unions can be persuaded to overcome their resistance to these innovations without exorbitant compensation for the loss in jobs, newspapers will establish themselves in the electronic publishing business; and it is not too far from there to go into electronic distribution as well.

Here is where European innovation is ahead of the United States. The British Post Office and the British broadcasting authorities have produced two different species of "teletext," or alphanumeric displays on television screens. The service is well suited to the presentation of classified advertisements and of financial information such as stock market results. Under protocols adopted by the British Post Office and likely to be copied elsewhere in Europe, newspapers could offer these traditional press services over the wired teletext system and charge subscribers who order them. Electronic composition of the print newspaper would make this very much easier.

Teletext is one of a family of new communications developments pressing on established institutions and confusing the conventional categories of print vs. electronic, mass media vs. point-to-point. Of these new technologies, only video discs and cassettes have escaped government control. Broadband cable in Western Europe is licensed or operated as part of the postal monopoly. Satellites are distant microwave stations and therefore fall under the same control. The flourishing private cable television industries of Canada and the United States are unknown in Western Europe, and there is nothing to compare with private satellite operation of the sort practiced—with U.S. government encouragement—by an AT&T, an RCA or an IBM. In Europe, the curtailment of private opportunity to offer these services has resulted in a much-lessened state of development.

When it comes to wired teletext, however, Western Europe may find room for private entrepreneurs. There are jurisdictional stalemates between broadcasting and telephone monopolies, and struggles for control over text editing between the broadcasting and newspaper industries. Furthermore, there is precedent for private operation: Computer service bureaus offer an analogous service for business users, and they have been authorized as private commercial entities.

This possibility of competitive entry into telecommunications is atypical. No competition is presently permitted for such things as telephone terminal equipment, specialized business services or satellite communications—all of which have been opened to competitive entry in the United States. Engineering predilection for a single, standardized telecommunications system has prevailed in Western Europe over economic or legal arguments in favor of encouraging technical and service innovation, just as the engineering profession dominates decision-making within the PTT's.

In broadcasting, some countries have opted for competition within a monopoly or oligopoly structure. Sweden has two separately programmed television networks, France three, Britain three, and West Germany two. In a number of these cases, however, the senior controlling authorities are the same people; when that is not the case, harmonization measures are taken to enforce diversity of programming even at the cost of decreased viewing audiences for one or another channel. Competition in this context is an instrument of control rather than openness.

There are significant departures from this theme. In the Netherlands, while the networks themselves are under uniform state control, programming on those networks is open to any group that can demonstrate (1) it has something to say and (2) it has a specified minimum number of members who share its social outlook—in practice, who subscribe to its program magazine. In Britain, the Annan Committee has proposed a somewhat comparable "open system" for the fourth television channel, to allow independent producers among others to have an outlet for their viewpoints. And in Italy, a series of mid-1970s decisions by its Supreme Constitutional Court have mandated open entry for both imported and local broadcasts, with the result that there are now roughly 100 local television stations plus 1000 local radio stations, which together can draw as much as half the prime-time audience away from RAI.

The Italian decrees were based on domestic constitutional guarantees of free speech. So was a recent French judicial decision, opening up local radio broadcasting to competitive entry despite the statutory monopoly over transmission held by an instrumentality of the RTF. The potential for expansion of those judgments into the legal framework of other West European countries and for their extension into other, broadcast-related, communications activities would seem to be pronounced. At the least, governments may find themselves drawn to consider the introduction of liberalizing reforms sufficient to ward off more extensive judicial revisions of their broadcasting systems.

To date there has been no disposition to promote cable as a competitive alternative to over-the-air broadcasting. A recent French regulation defines cable so as to exclude program origination, and the Annan Committee made no secret of its distaste for pay programming on cable. In West Germany and in Britain, as well as in France, cable is treated as a local service of limited utility whose expansion would entail unwelcome costs both for the national economy and for the national braodcasting system, which is supposed to impart the nation's cultural heritage in ways the government can assure.

Pluralism in video presentation is therefore as yet an unrealized ideal in most of Western Europe. Eventually the prices for video discs and video cassettes should decline to the point of making them as readily accessible to the public, or nearly so, as audio records are today. When that happens, the presentation of entertainment and of social views on the television screen should exhibit the same facility as that with which popular music groups now form, make records, dissolve, and reassemble to make records again. But those are free-market enterprises, not subject to government control. Pending the arrival on a commercial scale of new, unregulated services of this sort—which is not expected until some time in the 1990s—most West European governments are disposed to maintain present centralized structures rather than accede to new and more open ones.

In the main, West European governments are leery of relaxing controls on broadcasting, for fear that televison and to a lesser extent radio might usurp the political prerogatives of parliaments in the realms of debate and conciliation. It is thought necessary to contain the "dangerous power of arbitrage" that unelected broadcasters might wield, and a monopoly under government control is easier to control than a multiplicity of programming groups.

The formal controls over broadcasting content are similar to those in the United States. Programming is required to be balanced, objective, and impartial—very like the second part of the American "fairness doctrine." In Sweden the balance need not occur within the same program, and the younger commentators in both Sweden and West Germany are allowed subjective expressions of views that are not universally welcomed. Yet editorializing by broadcast management is generally not permitted. Subversive doctrines—dictatorship, racism, terrorism—are excluded from the balance requirement.

As for "equal time," in Western Europe this tends to take three forms. Sessions of Parliament, the legislative debates among the parties, are covered for the record; as yet there is very little live transmission, although BBC radio did begin regular afternoon broadcasting of the Question Period in the Spring of 1978. Ministers who ask for broadcasting time to make a political statement are subject to televised rebuttal by spokesmen for opposition parties. Beyond that there is the institution of the party political broadcast both during elections and more regularly throughout the year; time is usually allotted in accordance with electoral strength. The opportunity to make these appearances is evidently valued by politicians, despite probable audience apathy.

Violence and obscenity on television are treated with considerable maturity, through advisory notices and a recognition that it is up to the producer to resolve the inescapable tensions between creativity and audience sensitivities. The Annan Committee report on this issue is a model of sanity and sound judgment.

Informal controls over programming are much more significant, however, than the formal controls. In Britain these derive from the extraordinarily sweeping "reserve powers" in the BBC's license, permitting the government to dictate what shall and shall not be shown and even to take over the whole apparatus of broadcasting without recourse to Parliament. The powers have never been exercised as such, but they are thought to induce anticipatory compliance with substantive government policies on sensitive issues. In Sweden, comparable taboos have been imposed by the insistence of the "popular movements" represented on the board of Sveriges Radio. In France, and in Italy before the recent court decisions, the Latin tradition of political polarization causes the coverage of news and current affairs to reflect with some fidelity the views of the government in power. In West Germany, independence of expression is curtailed by the *proporz* system of political party appointments to key positions in the broadcasting stations.

These are all monopoly or oligopoly situations and the content controls, both formal and informal, are correspondingly stiff. In the Netherlands, where programming arrangements are pluralistic, content controls are much more relaxed. There is no balance or "fairness" requirement since a balance among contending viewpoints is built into the system. Offense against the security of the State or public order or morality can lead to suspension of broadcasting rights, but this has been leniently applied and under currently pending proposals could only follow a judicial judgment. The Dutch system is also hospitable to the work of free-lance producers, whose access to other West European broadcasting institutions has been steadily declining.

The "Open Broadcasting Authority" proposed by the Annan Committee would be similarly receptive to independent producers and would likewise relax controls over content. Balance could be attained over time, as in Sweden, and at least some of the responsibility for programs would be shifted from the Authority to the producers. There is a certain cloudiness in the Annan Committee descriptions of exactly what would happen, but then this is a new idea for Britain.

The respective claims of pluralism and paternalism, and of old and new, are also involved in the treatment of Citizens' Band radio. This is a form of personalized communications allowing individuals to "broadcast" into the ether for the purpose of holding point-to-point conversations. It makes extravagant claims on the frequency spectrum in comparison with other mobile and personalized services such as radio paging. But it is also a very democratic mode of discourse in its admission of participants and in its lack of censorship or mediation of what is said. Most West European governments have stressed its wastefulness and disorganized character. They have been unwilling to subtract frequencies from oligopoly broadcasting or otherwise to open up very much room for the diversity of CB service.

Another traditional service that is under siege from new technological developments is the postal service. Electronic alternatives already with us (like computer conferencing), and others that will shortly be introduced (like interconnected magnetic-card typewriters), can deliver business and eventually personal messages faster, more frequently and cheaper than conventional mail delivery. The technical and economic aspects of the likely shift over are being examined internally by the post and telegraph administrations of Western Europe, but there is very little published discussion of either economic or social consequences. Although posts and telecommunications both come under the same roof in Europe, it is not clear that the losses on one side of the house will be made up by gains on the other; and it does seem likely that there will be serious transitional strains, which call for advanced planning.

What "electronic mail" could do to the mails, "electronic publishing" might eventually do to some parts of the print press. Newspaper proprietors have moved to protect themselves by, among other things, seeking a prescriptive right to participation in ownership and management of the wired teletext medium. The British Royal Commission on the Press turned that down. But there seems no question that the press can participate as electronic information suppliers and even as competitive operators of computer-retrieval or teletext systems. The real issue is what measures may be called for to protect the interests of readers. On that question there is as yet no public discussion at all.

It is a confusing time for analysts and planners. The old categories are breaking down. The KtK recognized the emergence of what it termed a "technical transmission integration" and said that it calls into question the adequacy of present organizational structures; but it thought this was a political question on which it should offer no advice. The Annan Committee was similarly unwilling to take a position on the need for closer coordination of governmental policy units. Since the blurring of borders between the various services was, in its view, a process that will take 15 years to complete, the politics of government reorganization could be left to the Prime

Minister's discretion; although—in a memorable phrase—"eventually Governments will have to face the problem of communications policy." The Carter Committee was also hesitant to take anything that might be judged a political initiative. It conceded the need for a long-term communications strategy to deal with message distribution of all kinds, but it proposed to leave this to a citizens' advisory council.

The reticence of these inquiry committees in grappling with what Alvin Toffler has called "Future Shock" is the reflection of a somewhat closeted approach to policy planning in Western Europe. There is no independent regulatory forum to serve as a catalyst for new perceptions about established industry and governmental structures. Policy is arrived at largely behind institutional doors and without the involvement of the public or the participation of knowledgeable outsiders. Communications policy competence is fragmented among a variety of ministries—broadcasting in one place, posts and telecommunications in another, the press in a third—with no coordinating mechanism to draw them together. The arrival of a new technology or service typically precipitates a struggle over which ministry shall control it, rather than a questioning of whether existing lines of responsibility are appropriate. This makes for short-range vision, not long-range or comprehensive planning.

European legislatures could supply the deficiency but they do not. Party loyalties have been so tightened that majority members are loath to criticize their ministerial colleagues or even to go very far to encourage constructive change. Most parliamentary committees have a very general jurisdiction that precludes careful examination of communications policy, and continuing oversight of the sort practiced by committees of the U.S. Congress is not done. Still less are there "foresight" responsibilities of the kind adopted in 1974 by the U.S. House of Representatives for its committees. More basically, those politicians who care about the subject recognize a need for systematic schooling in its intricacies. At present, briefings are available only from industrialists and civil servants and other interested parties, which does not allow the formation of confidently independent judgments.

The West European judiciary does not participate routinely in the declaration or elaboration of national communications policy. They are not called upon, as are their American counterparts, to review on a regular basis the rules and decisions adopted by an independent regulatory agency. But when they do enter the area, it can be in a very important way. In 1961 the Federal Constitutional Court in West Germany upheld the constitutionality of a public broadcasting monopoly. In 1960 the Italian Supreme Constitutional Court did the same thing, then turned around in 1974 and 1976 to require liberalization of the RAI and open entry for local and foreign broadcasts. Most recently, a lower French court has followed that lead. The Italian decrees were very wideranging, embracing technical and economic judgments of a dubious validity and dictating a political charter of rights and responsibilities in what Americans would likely consider an anti-democratic manner. But intervention of this character may have been necessary to free the workings of a political democracy stalemated between rival parties and therefore unable to carry through needed reforms. And the courts in all three of the countries under discussion were interpreting free-speech provisions in their national constitutions. In these limited circumstances, where there is no visible alternative to judicial activism, the courts may continue to have an important role to play.

But the judiciary cannot be counted on to exhibit comparable solicitude for other important values in communications policy, and by its nature the process of adjudication looks to redress of past wrongs rather than anticipation of future needs. Advisory groups of two kinds have been used or proposed to fill in the gaps. One are advisory councils of a continuing nature, some proposed by the Annan and Carter Committees and some—like the Haut Conseil de l'Audiovisuel—already in existence. To be effective, these need not only very good people and a suitably wide mandate, but also a presently lacking commitment by politicians to the furtherance of their work. The other sort are the committees of inquiry themselves, which as we have seen are hesitant about reaching into the future or across industry lines. This is not strictly speaking their failing. It was the British government, not the three British committees, that chose to look separately into broadcasting, telecommunications and the press. And it is the French government that has thus far withheld encouragement for long-range or comprehensive policy analysis from the Haut Conseil.

These constraints stem from an insistence on retaining political control. They reflect an underlying paternalism, which is the dominant feature of West European communications policymaking. The few decide for the many, and without inviting any outside those few into the policy councils. There are some losses—in openness, in participation, in public engagement—but there is not much complaint. It seems to be widely recognized and accepted that decisions are being taken in pursuit of important values. These include order, stability and avoidance of waste. Quality is a very important consideration, in terms both of engineering design and of cultural merit; and these are matters that cannot be decided by popular preference.

Americans would probably criticize European policymaking on several grounds: It does not foster service innovation or economic efficiency, it unnecessarily restricts consumers' freedom of choice, and it does not allow democratic involvement in the decision process. Europeans, on the other hand, would criticize the Americans for a wasteful insistence on both market competition and procedural regularity, claiming that each glorifies a process instead of the end result. What is wanted, they would say, is high quality and wise judgment—each of which can be better produced by an elite.

There is no point in debating the relative merits of these two positions or in seeking to reconcile them. Each springs from a cultural and social and political history. Elitism is the outgrowth of a class system that still persists today even in those West European societies whose governments call themselves Social Democratic. Populism arises from the experience of those European settlers of North America who were seeking to broaden the boundaries of personal freedom. Neither system is readily translatable from one side of the ocean to the other, but there are features of each that on patient examination may have more cross-relevance and utility for the future than they have been accorded up till now.

II
Institutional
and Industry Structure

A. Posts and Telecommunications (PTT)

Throughout Western Europe, the business of point-to-point communications—mail, telephone, telegraph, telex, data transmission, mobile radio—is run as an integrated monopoly under state control. The arrangement is an historic one, dating back to the era of post roads and country inns from which the modern concept of the common carrier emerged. The royal or imperial privilege conferred on national postal monopolies of the 17th century has evolved into the statutory monopoly for posts and telecommunications of today.

1. *Governmental management.*   There are some variations on the present structural theme: In France, for example, the PTT is operated as a government department under direct management by the politically responsible minister; in Spain and Italy there is private share ownership in, but still government control of, the PTT; and in Britain and Sweden the PTT is an independent state corporation with its own board and management appointed by and responsive to the relevant minister. In all cases state control of telecommunications is more pervasive than in the United States.

The scope of the monopoly is wide-ranging. Anything that relates immediately to the provision of public point-to-point message service falls as a general matter under monopoly control. The PTT monopolies stop short, however, of telecommunications equipment manufacturing. In theory, the European PTT's contract com-

15

petitively for their equipment. They do not have an integrated supplier relationship such as that existing between the Bell System and Western Electric. In practice, as agents or instrumentalities of their governments, the PTT's tend to display a close contractual solicitude for the welfare of their domestic manufacturing firms.

From a North American point of view, perhaps the most notable fact about the European PTT's is the total absence of any independent regulatory authority. Rates and service conditions are not subject to the kind of public accountability made familiar in the United States and Canada by the FCC and the CRTC. There is, moreover, no detached forum for the resolution of inter-industry disputes over the provision of the newer forms of electronic service—broadband cable, for example, or teletext.

All decisions are taken instead by a process of administrative determination within the PTT's. Very often they are made by career civil servants with a penchant towards the safe and the familiar. Even when the PTT has been turned into an independent state corporation, as in Britain, the influence on its employees of the civil service outlook can be expected to persist for another generation or two. And in such cases a new question arises: the proper relationship between political control and business management.

2. *Business judgment.*   After the 1969 legislation giving it a form of independence, the British Post Office gained a status similar to that of other nationalized industries. Its minister, now the Secretary of State for Industry, exercises authority through appointments to the Board, review and approval of total investment and borrowing, and the giving of what are usually general instructions. The Carter Committee thought it proper to question whether this arm's-length relationship is adequate to the governance of a monopoly—one with captive customers and a business that cannot be allowed to fail. Its answer was to recommend the splitting up of the company under two separate Boards, for Postal Business and for Telecommunications Business, and the establishment as a bridging mechanism of an independent Council on Post Office and Telecommunications Affairs to advise the Secretary of State—who would gain more specific and more flexible powers of direction in the bargain.

But this merely highlighted the unsettled nature of the relationship between supervision of a business and its management. The Carter Committee, for example, recommended that the Secretary of State *impose* a short-run marginal pricing scheme on competitive mail services and *fix* standards of telephone service, matters which in the United States would be dealt with by pricing floors and standards criteria. The Committee admitted to the lack of prior guidance in the matter:

> As between Government and the Post Office there is no clear and agreed understanding about those policy matters in which it may be appropriate for Government to intervene and those executive management matters in which it is not appropriate.[5]

The absence of such understanding tends to diminish the difference between the PTT's that are independent in form and those that are integrated into a government ministry. All meet together with some regularity in the Conférence Européenne des Postes et Télécommunications (CEPT) for the harmonization of policies. All may be considered essentially state-run monopolies.

This very likely has consequences outside the field of point-to-point communications. The PTT's provide the telecommunications links for broadcasting and issue the licenses for that service. The strong tradition of public monopolies in the one case may well have influenced the industry structure in the second.

B. Broadcasting

1. *Governmental superintendence.* In the United States, public broadcasting came as an afterthought, whereas in Western Europe it was the first and is still usually the only thought. The typical European structure features a monopoly or (as with independent broadcasting in Britain) a duopoly authorized by the State. One or more broadcasting entities are established to exercise that authority and are licensed by the PTT, with license agreements or "cahiers des charges" detailing the broadcast organizations' rights and duties. The responsible minister holds large and often ambiguous powers. The Chairman of the Governing Board and/or the Director General of the broadcasting entity is chosen by this minister.

Political selection of personnel sometimes goes well beyond the senior management level. In West Germany, for example, there is an entrenched system of *proporz*, whereby broadcasting-station producers and editors and even journalists are appointed in proportion to the local electoral strength of their respective political parties. A similar system has recently evolved in Italy. It is explained by knowledgeable European observers as an outgrowth of the post-Weimar Republic thirst for strong and stable political parties; others question the need for *proporz* now that such parties have been established, and some suggest that broadcasting in these circumstances should become a countervailing, independent force.[6] But *proporz* continues.

The question of independence also arises with the system of financing for European public television. It is based on annual license fees, which are levied on radio and television receivers. The scheme appears to work efficiently and to generate the needed revenues, but in an inflationary era it depends upon the frequent willingness of governments to propose, and parliaments to approve, increases in the individual rates and total fees. This is liable to diminish to some degree the margin of political independence that the broadcasting organizations can exercise. It is noteworthy that when public broadcasting was being introduced in the United States in 1967, a license-fee system for its financing was rejected by the U.S. Treasury.

The U.S. and Canada, of course, have established independent regulatory commissions as a way of seeking an arm's-length relationship between broadcasting and government. Decisions are made on an open record after adversary hearings and on the basis of pre-established (though often murky) standards for judgment. Yet West Europeans have declined to adopt this model, in part because they claim it would lead to government over-reaching. The Annan Committee in Britain, for example, dismissed the notion of a central Broadcasting Commission or Council on the ground that it would be likely to intrude into programming, inject politics into broadcasting practices and move monopoly power into government.[7]

2. *Commercial influence*. This spirited defense of the *status quo* strongly implies that European broadcasting is currently free from governmental over-reaching. In part this is a question of image: The BBC asserts an independent judgment, and the public tends to accept that at face value. But in part the question goes a great deal deeper and helps to explain the primacy of public television. The task of the State is seen as one of protecting freedom of expression from capture by commercial interests. The government

at least purports to act for the State, which is to say the interest of the public generally. It may abuse that trust from time to time, but those risks are apparently more comfortable to bear than the risk of commercial usurpation for what are seen as narrowly selfish ends.[8]

To be sure, commercial television has made its appearance in Europe, through bloc advertising at the beginning and end and at "natural breaks" in programs. In most European countries advertising is still deliberately a minor factor: It supplies only six percent of net revenues for the West German stations,[9] while in the Netherlands it is handled by a separate foundation and is limited to a maximum of 15 minutes per network per day.[10] But there is an important commercial network, ITV, in Britain, and a complex system of commercial advertising on two of the three public networks in France. The way in which those two commercial systems have evolved suggests an uneasy balance between market-competition objectives and the satisfaction of centrally determined tastes.

ITV was introduced in Britain in 1955 as an antidote to what some saw as a certain smugness in the BBC. Together with its commercial-radio counterpart, it was intended to make the broadcasting establishment aware of, and responsive to, public desires for light entertainment. ITV has to cater to mass tastes in order to garner the advertising dollar. The BBC cannot afford to slip too far in the ratings either, for fear its license fees might be cut. Accordingly, it has increased its offerings of popular music, series drawn from everyday life and Hollywood films. But the competitive pull also operates in the other direction. The BBC had enjoyed a monopoly for two generations, and its standards of quality were ingrained in public expectations. ITV and commercial radio have had to cater "upwards" to these tastes, with the result that many of its programs are of high quality.

Since the 1960s, the BBC has had two television networks with which to confront the ITV challenge. It has used them quite deliberately for counter-programming: When a serious subject such as opera or a political party conference is on one network, a light program such as a sports event or a music hall is on the other. This allows them to keep pace with ITV in either direction, and to offer viewers a choice at all times.

ITV is unlikely to be given a comparable opportunity. In the debate over a fourth channel, it has thus far found few supporters for its desire to be given supervisory control. The Annan Committee, which considered this issue at length, reported "we are all agreed" that the fourth channel "should not develop into another competitive channel whose programmes are aimed at mass audiences or a channel which for most of the time is ITV 2."[11] So it appears that in England commercial broadcasting is, as a matter of present policy, confined to a limited and secondary place.

The situation in France deserves brief exposition. Following a history of maladministration, cost overruns and crippling strikes in the old ORTF, the new Giscard administration in 1974 pushed through Parliament a series of structural and operating reforms. Transmission was separated from programming and handed over to a new state monopoly, TDF, which was also given responsibility for technical research and development. Another new corporation, SFP, was established as a production enterprise under French company law, one of whose tasks was to create programming for three of the four newly separated but still government-owned networks: Radio-France, TéléFrance I, Antenne 2, and France Régions 3. Of these, the television networks were obliged to buy a decreasing minimum proportion of their programs from SFP. They were also obliged to take a minimum of 30 hours of experimental programming from INA, the Institut National de l'Audiovisuel, which was given a research as well as a training and archival function.[12]

Thus far the seven corporations of the newly decentralized RTF (Radiodiffusion et Télévision Française) would seem to be linked together by a continuing centralized direction. But the entire system depends on the financing that is generated by the broadcasting networks, and this is in turn dependent on commercial advertising.[13] In 1977, the RTF companies divided among themselves overall revenues of some 3,600 million francs, of which 65.7 percent came from license fees and 26.4 percent from advertising. These figures actually understate the degree of advertising dependence: For TFI and A2, the only two television networks that engage in brand advertising, income from this source represented 61.5 and 50.7 percent, respectively, of their budgets. The incentives would seem very strong for each network to reach for the largest possible share of the audience.

There is, however, a distribution formula for license-fee income that complicates the picture. It is composed one part of audience size and three parts of program quality. The quality index is made up by polls taken among viewers, plus a grading system devised by a quality control commission of 27 members appointed by the Haut Conseil de l'Audiovisuel—a consultative body of distinguished citizens. The whole process is costly and time-consuming, as it moves through yet another commission of five judges appointed by the Conseil d'Etat and the Cour des Comptes. And the resulting reallocations of income are very minor. In 1977, TF I dropped Fr. 1.5 million below what it would have received without a distribution formula; A2 dropped Fr. 6.6 million; FR 3 gained Fr. 6.9 million; and Radio-France gained Fr. 1.2 million. By contrast, the costs of operating the distribution formula in 1977 were Fr. 13.3 million. Even more significantly, funds transfers ordered by the government without reference to the formula totalled Fr. 111.2 million.[14]

It is difficult to know what effect, if any, this income redistribution pattern has on programming incentives. It could be that the lure of advertising revenue remains strong, and that programming for mass tastes on something like the American model results. The French understandably pride themselves on disseminating their own cultural heritage, and they point to import figures showing that no more than nine percent of their programs originate from outside France. Yet a look at the prime-time "picks" of the most widely circulated magazine in France, *Télé 7 Jours*, for a randomly selected week in early 1978, discloses that of the 34 programs recommended, nine are shows or films from the United States and one is from Italy: roughly one-third of the total.[15] The catering to mass tastes appears marked.

Yet such tendencies could be on the wane. They have been firmly criticized by the Finance Committee of the National Assembly, in its 1977 report on the RTF.[16] The government has deemed excessive TF I's dependence on advertising revenue and ordered it reduced in 1978. The Haut Conseil de l'Audiovisuel has gone further and informally recommended the institution of programming harmonization among the three broadcasting networks, on what sounds very like the model of the BBC. And the very same issue of *Télé 7 Jours* announced that the presidents of the three television networks had in fact met and devised a scheme of regular consultation to avoid competitive offerings of the same genre of programs. As editorialized by this magazine, which owes its own success entirely to market forces, the overriding object of such harmonization should be "la qualité"—even though to achieve it will require centralized agreements to resist market forces.[17]

3. *Structures of autonomy: (a)* DECENTRALIZATION.   If European broadcasting organizations have found ways of resisting undue commercial influence, some have also found various protective arrangements against excessive intrusion by centralized government authority. In West Germany, this is done by a provision of the Basic Law assigning to the States, or Länder, the responsibility for organizing and regulating broadcast transmission. The nine German television broadcasting stations exist by virtue of their individual or interstate agreements with the Länder. There are two national networks, but each is subject to this basic arrangement. The first, ARD, is a membership organization put together by the stations, while the second, ZDF, was created by agreement among all the Länder.

Undoubtedly, the German broadcasting structure owes much to the experiences of World War II and the strong desire to prevent reemergence of a centralized propaganda apparatus.[18] In its creation of independent public corporations, the German system was also influenced by the model of the BBC. That the stations are public-service organizations, and not private commercial enterprises, was the holding of a landmark decision by the Federal Constitutional Court in 1961. This came against the background of a long-standing and still continuing, but so far unsuccessful, effort on the part of certain newspaper publishers and others to gain approval for a rival system of commercial broadcasting. The Constitutional Court decided, in effect, that Germany could opt for an exclusively public system without having to subject that system to centralized government direction or control.[19]

There have been movements, thus far inconclusive, towards a comparable regional dispersal of broadcasting in other West European countries. France Régions 3 is supposed to be a regional network, but its programming that actually bears this character covers only 35 minutes in the early evening and there is no devolution of authority towards the provinces. The Swedish Committee on Broadcasting recommended in 1977 that Sveriges Radio be reorganized so as to have one regional television network with production facilities decentralized into nine regions, each with its own audience council to advise on programming; this has been strongly criticized, on grounds of both cost and quality, and it is unlikely to be adopted. Finally, the Annan Committee proposed to take authority over local broadcasting away from the BBC and IBA and to vest it in a new Local Broadcasting Authority—which would, however, be another centralized institution. To date, West Germany stands alone in Western Europe with an effectively decentralized broadcasting structure.[20]

(b) BUFFER GROUPS. Sweden has found other ways to resist excessive centralized government control. Broadcasting is conducted through a state-controlled monopoly, Sveriges Radio, which is financed through license fees, but there are several distinctive provisions. First, ownership is divided into private hands: business groups, the print press, and overwhelmingly the so-called "popular movements" which hold 60 percent of the shares; these movements consist of important social groupings like the temperance and evangelical movements, consumers' associations and the labor movement. Second, the Board of Directors is made up of 13 members. The government appoints the chairman plus only five other directors, leaving a majority of the board to be chosen by the shareholders (five members) and the employees (two). Third, the programming affairs of the corporation are distributed among seven separate entities: radio broadcasting, TV network 1, TV network 2, Swedish regions, Central News Service, External Broadcasting and Educational Broadcasting.[21]

Thus, while the duties of Sveriges Radio are spelled out in acts of Parliament and in periodic agreements with the Government, the implementation of those duties is entrusted to a structure with built-in checks against day-to-day governmental encroachment.

Perhaps more important still are the tools by which both the press and broadcasting in Sweden can intrude into governmental affairs. Elsewhere in Europe, broadcast criticism of governments is muted, and free-swinging investigative broadcast journalism is little known. (It bears recalling in this connection that the *Washington Post* and the *New York Times*, not the American television networks, broke open the Pentagon Papers and Watergate affairs.) In Sweden the situation is, at least in theory, entirely different. Journalists in broadcasting feel they enjoy the same freedom, or even more, than their colleagues in the print press. And Swedes have been proud of it.

This situation could change. It arose under the prolonged political domination of one party, the Social Democrats, in a period of economic prosperity and social harmony. In 1966, the last Social Democratic Prime Minister, Olof Palme, who was then Minister of Posts and Telecommunications, voiced the ideal in a parliamentary debate when he urged his colleagues at all cost to "guard the right of television to openly criticize society, the authorities, and private financial interest."[22] Since that time Sweden has experienced its share of student and left-wing unrest, some terrorist acts, a large influx of immigrants, economic recession, and now the advent of a Conservative Government. It is not certain that the new "authorities" will at all times exhibit the previous tolerance towards criticism from the television journalists.

Those journalists have had available to them what is probably the most far-reaching Freedom of Information Act in the world. While in other Western countries official restrictions on disclosing certain kinds of sensitive information are quite extensive, in Sweden they are virtually non-existent. Furthermore, the agreement between the State and Sveriges Radio specifies that extensive freedom of expression and information shall prevail on radio and television. It seems unreal, and to a degree it is.

For in practice, it must be noted, Swedish television journalists observe certain informal taboos, arising from personal friendships with politicians, from respect for cherished social institutions, and possibly from fear of government exercise of its power over finance. In the course of the 1976 election campaign, for example, Sveriges Radio carried stories of the series of scandals that rocked the Social Democrats, just as the newspapers did; but it conducted no extensive research of its own, and presented no documentary programs on the issue of governmental corruption. In fact, investigative journalism is not something for which the Swedish government has seen fit to budget adequately. And Swedish broadcasting carries almost no political satire.[23]

The reason for this latter limitation probably relates to the self-importance of the interest groups that make up the "popular movements" so heavily represented among Sveriges Radio's shareholders and on its Board. These groups take themselves quite seriously and do not hesitate to intrude into questions of programming.[24] Even if such "intrusions" are resisted, as they evidently are, they are bound to exert a restraining influence on what would otherwise be the exercise of freedoms wrested from government. It appears that Swedish broadcasting may have expanded its autonomy in one direction only to have foreshortened it in another.

(c) ACCESS PROGRAMMING.   In the Netherlands, by contrast, a unique broadcasting system has been devised to use the self-interest of affiliation groups in the service of maximum diversity and freedom.[25] The two television channels are owned and controlled by the government. But their use is awarded to, and license fees are shared among, a group of private, non-profit, membership organizations that span a full gamut of political and social thought: AVRO (conservative), EO (fundamentalist), KRO (Catholic), NCRV (Calvinist), TROS (neutral), VARA (Socialist), VOO (neutral) and VPRO (non-conformist). Together these groups own a 50 percent share in the Netherlands Broadcasting Foundation (NOS), which provides studio facilities and also originates its own programming of general interest: news, sports, Eurovision, etc. This leaves the affiliation groups to beam their own messages to their members and to others who may tune them in; a union member may sample the conservative programs, for example, along with those in the Socialist time slot, just as a Catholic may watch Calvinist programming if he chooses.[26]

This system had its origin in the 19th century struggle for social and political equality in the Netherlands. First the Catholics and the Calvinists, later the Socialists, gained the right to establish their own schools—subsidized by the State—and their own hospitals, relief and recreational organizations, employee associations and the rest. This was the system in place when radio broadcasting came along, and it was readily applied to the new service. But there was a difference: Where the earlier arrangements operated to insulate the social groups from each other, broadcasting, reaching into every home, offered the opportunity of unifying society.

Probably the various groups saw radio and then television as means to emphasize their own worth and dignity, as well as to reach across social barriers to attract new members to their cause. At its best, this system doubtless produced, and on occasion still produces, an ideal representation of that "marketplace of ideas" identified in Anglo-American political history with Milton, Mill and Holmes. There is the richness of diversity and the solidity of common aims. A genuine pluralism serves to ward off both governmental interference and commercial exploitation while giving the public a choice of competing philosophies.

Yet the system bore within itself the seeds of its own deterioration. In part, it succeeded too well. Social emancipation for the Catholics, Calvinists, Socialists and others was achieved. The missionary urge was in time followed by a desire not to offend. The programming mix, having been heady, became bland. (It must be said that VPRO has not succumbed. Whether documenting the Nazi past of a newly designated NATO military commander or introducing for the first time a naked woman—later, naked men—to the screen, VPRO has remained faithful to its irreverent origins.)

In part, as well, the Dutch pluralistic system has been undermined by its own mechanisms. These provide for entry into programming by any organization that can claim 40,000 members. Such a group gets one hour of television a week and can add another hour and a half if its membership after two years rises to 100,000. Larger time allowances are made available to groups of 250,000 members and still more when the membership reaches 400,000—up to a maximum present allocation of eight hours and 20 minutes of broadcasting time. In practice, membership figures are calculated on the basis of subscriptions to the organization's weekly program guide.

The spirit of the law, if not its letter, required that in order to get transmission time a group had to demonstrate both (1) that it had something to say and (2) that it was supported by a certain number of people. The authorization of VOO (neutral) was at first held up by the relevant minister because it failed to meet the first criterion, but he was overruled on legal grounds within the government. (Ironically, VOO has thus far failed to advance beyond "candidate" status because fewer than half of its 100,000 members were found to be paying the license fee.) VOO, like TROS before it, was a pirate broadcaster. The chairman of TROS cheerfully admitted it had nothing to say: "The essence is to give to the people the programmes they want to see. So, no politics. I say to the viewers: we are here for you, not for ourselves. The viewer is the boss. So often I hear viewers saying to me: I am glad you do not irritate us."

TROS has been very successful with programming aimed at the lowest common denominator. Sales of its program guide have soared. This success has triggered a competition for ratings throughout the system (always excepting VPRO). The result, called "trossification" by the Dutch, has been to narrow quite substantially the diversity of programming and to lower the standards of its quality.[27] To be sure, the decline must be seen in relative terms:

Freedom of expression is still a strong tradition, the access scheme for differing social groups is still by far the most adventurous in the world, and the continuing inventiveness of at least one group suggests that Dutch broadcasting has not lost its horizon-opening potential. But the structural scheme in the Netherlands is not at present living up to its former promise.

(d) OPEN ENTRY. There is one last structural path to broadcasting autonomy in Europe, and that is open entry. This is the situation in Italy, though not through political or legislative choice. In a series of decisions in the middle 1970s, the Italian Constitutional Court mandated both that the existing state monopoly be liberalized and that the way be opened to essentially unlimited entry by foreign broadcasts, national cable systems and local broadcasters.[28]

Before 1974 the Italian system was quite straightforward. There was a state broadcasting monopoly, RAI, with exclusive authority to transmit radio and television programs. This arrangement had been held to be constitutional in 1960, on the same ground as was used to uphold the limitation on the number of broadcasters who could operate in the United States, namely the scarcity of available bandwidth. Various governmental committees were created in Italy to supervise program planning and political objectivity, but the net effect was to leave real authority with the Prime Minister, who also appointed the RAI General Manager. Since the Christian Democrats remained in power throughout the postwar period, this party was content to leave the system basically untouched from 1947 to 1975.

In 1974, however, the Constitutional Court issued three judgments that created a necessity for legislative reform.[29] In the first, the Court ruled that municipal cable systems do not interfere with use of over-the-air frequencies and are therefore exempt from the government monopoly; for financial and economic reasons cable has not since developed into a viable industry in Italy and so this decision had no immediate practical effect. In the second, the Court held (virtually in passing) that foreign broadcasters, operating on frequencies different from those assigned by international agreement to Italy, do not interfere with RAI's operations—with the result that retransmission stations within Italy could not be barred by the government. This did have practical consequences, as we shall see.

In a third judgment the Court went much further and ruled

that its 1960 validation of the state broadcasting monopoly could only be sustained if the operation of that monopoly met certain specified conditions. In what Americans would likely call an advisory or gratuitous opinion, the Court laid down what amounted to a brand new charter for RAI. The conditions were these:

(1) The administration of RAI should not be entirely or mainly a reflection of the government in power (as it clearly had been);

(2) There must be a guarantee of the impartiality of news programs (which had been essentially an outlet for government orthodoxy);

(3) Effective control over the service must be given to Parliament (which had been effectively excluded);

(4) There must be a fostering of the objectivity and professionalism of journalists (who had been politicized through the appointment power);

(5) Advertising must be restricted;

(6) Arrangements must be made to provide and govern access;

(7) There must be guarantees for the rights of the individual.

It is difficult to know how much of this "charter" was prompted by the case or the parties and how much represented the Court's own dismay at the existing broadcasting structure. But the new charter made reform imperative, and the Government moved quickly to reach agreement with the other political parties on a reform law. As embodied in Law No. 103 of April 14, 1975, the changes were far-reaching. Effective power over RAI was shifted to a Parliamentary Commission with 40 members chosen in proportion to party power. The Board of RAI-TV was given 16 members, with a majority of 10 chosen by this Parliamentary Commission. (Proportional representation on a major scale, what some have dubbed *ultra-proporz*, thereupon established itself in the various RAI divisions previously controlled exclusively by the party in power.) The authority of the General Manager was curtailed. The Parliamentary Commission was empowered to examine and approve access applications. Editors of news programs were given autonomous status by legislation, making them formally equivalent to newspaper editors.

During this period other things had been happening outside the political and judicial arenas. Pirate broadcasting operations had been started and were thriving on weak and inconsistent enforcement of the RAI monopoly law. On July 20, 1976, in its decision

No. 202, the Constitutional Court moved to give these operations a never-before-enjoyed legitimacy. The Court held unconstitutional that part of Law No. 103 forbidding competition insofar as broadcasting within a "local radius" is concerned. In effect it dusted off its decision respecting cable television and applied it to this circumstance. But in contrast to that earlier decision, the effects have been immediate and extensive.

According to a recent account, there are now roughly 100 private television stations in Italy and about 1000 private radio stations.[30] Some of these are commercially sponsored while others are ideological in their backing and output—some Communist, some Catholic, some other. The Minister of Posts has defined "local" for purposes of the Court's decision as operating within a maximum radius of 15 kilometers and reaching no more than 100,000 viewers or listeners. This would certainly make it difficult to sustain commercial operation. But it would not curtail ideological operations. And the limitation does not address the syndicating of programs among even very small stations. Recent figures suggest that the private radio stations are now taking almost 50 percent of the prime-time audiences away from the RAI.[31]

Since the 1974 Court decision, moreover, foreign broadcasts have been received extensively in Italy. These include transmissions from stations in Monte Carlo, Lugano, and Capodistria in Yugoslavia—again, perhaps, the ideological touch—as well as the regular French television broadcasts. Italian advertising has migrated to some of these stations, attracted by competitive rates. An estimated two-thirds of all Italian television sets are positioned to receive at least one foreign broadcast and perhaps half of these do, in fact, receive them.[32]

To deal with this state of unplanned anarchy, the government must submit and maneuver through Parliament yet another reform law. The balance of political forces between the Christian Democrats and the Communists currently clouds the prospects for agreement on so quintessentially political a subject as open vs. closed entry into broadcasting. So Italy may involuntarily become a laboratory for the study of an open system of entry.

Under more controlled conditions, Sweden has recently chosen to try a similar experiment with very local broadcasting. Following the 1976 election, the "popular movements" and others have been authorized to operate local transmitters with the limited power to reach five kilometers. In this case, the principle is probably more important than the current practice.

Finally, in France a recent lower court decision has reached a judgment very similar to that of the Italian Constitutional Court. In this case it seems clearly to have resulted from a deliberate political step, since the challenge was brought by a group of lawyers, one of whom is a member of President Giscard d'Estaing's central party committee. This group established a private radio station, Radio Fil Bleu, and publicized it widely. TDF, the State transmission monopoly, sought to close it down. The court declined, stating that the RTF law is subordinate to the French Constitution's provisions for liberty of expression and information and also to the European Convention on Human Rights. The decision is currently on appeal.[33]

Conceivably these straws in the wind may suggest an eventual European retreat from broadcasting monopoly, at least in countries outside the Netherlands, and the adoption of some sort of pluralistic access arrangements. This would be one way, perhaps not the only way, of warding off governmental interference in programming. If that turns out to be the case, Italian politicians will have found themselves dragged into the vanguard.

C.   The Press

There are no entry restrictions on the West European press and no systematic governmental interference with print journalism.[34] In this area, in the main, Adam Smith's "invisible hand" is allowed to operate and is expected, through the market competition of ideas and entertainment, to serve both the public and the private interest.

1. *Subsidies.*   There are various subsidy schemes and preferential tax arrangements that could make newspapers dependent on their governments, but this seems not to have happened. In France, West Germany, the Netherlands and Sweden tax and postal concessions are available to all newspapers, with no central agency to make potentially invidious choices. The Royal Commission on the Press, in Britain, recently shied away from such arrangements on the grounds that they were expensive and could provide aid to non-needy publications. (Yet as its report also conceded, British newspapers and magazines now get an across-the-

board exemption from value-added tax worth 60 million pounds a year.) The Commission in any event preferred to avoid any system that might lead to governmental assistance premised on the editorial policies of particular newspapers.[35]

In practice there seems little evidence of such a risk. In Sweden, for example, where the newspapers have long aligned themselves with political parties, loan and subsidy schemes are tied to a showing of financial need. The formulae used are automatic in operation, e.g., a production subsidy based on newsprint consumed for editorial material and paid to newspapers with less than 40 percent household penetration in any of the markets designated by an independent Newspaper Support Board. In this way, fully 32 daily and another 32 weekly newspapers are assisted; each gets about 20 percent of its total income in this fashion. None of these papers appears to have compromised its editorial freedom and the full play of partisan viewpoints continues to flourish.[36]

2. *Self-regulation.* But whether through subsidy arrangements or otherwise, European newspapers are expected to have a point of view and to express it. Apart from journalistic ethics, there is no legal requirement of fairness or balance in newspaper coverage. The press serves an advocacy function for various viewpoints, and one journal's set of opinions is supposed to be offset by others, with no need for governments to referee the contest.

The European press employs various measures of self-regulation, of which one sort is typified by the British Press Council. That body, which has been in existence for 25 years, at first had a membership drawn only from the profession. Among the Council's objectives was the consideration of complaints from the public, but its impartiality was doubted and lay members were progressively added until the most recent Royal Commission recommended that the Council appoint an equal number of lay and press members and an independent chairman. Charges of damage to reputation and of misrepresentation have been heard by the Council as an alternative to litigation, with the complainant obliged to waive legal action before the Council would entertain his case. There is reason to doubt the propriety of this requirement, and the recent Royal Commission has proposed that thought be given to its abolition.

Perhaps the most pointed criticism of the British Press Council, beyond its slowness in hearing cases and affording relief, has been for its failure to draw up a written code of conduct for journalists out of its past, largely unexplained, adjudications. It remains to be seen how far the Council will wish to move in this direction. In the United States, some journalists' associations have reached good-faith agreements with the bar on steps to harmonize the ideal of a free press with that of a fair trial—only to find their voluntary "codes" taken over by the courts and used as a measure of judicial regulation rather than self-regulation. The same process of institutionalization could take place with a written code of conduct.

Other countries have taken other approaches.[37] West Germany has legislated a right of reply similar to that ruled unconstitutional by the U.S. Supreme Court in the *Miami Herald* case. Sweden has a Press Ombudsman, a judge, who investigates complaints and decides which to submit to the Swedish Press Council. There is as yet not enough experience with either system to determine whether it will intrude unduly on the independence of the press.

3. *Oligopoly.*   Threats to a free and diverse press have also arisen out of the industry in the form of progressive concentration of ownership and control. This should not be overstated. European countries are small enough and sufficiently accustomed to cultural domination by the major metropolitan centers to have a genuinely competitive national press. In Britain, where the provincial papers are monopolies, there are nine national Sunday newspapers (of which three are considered "quality" and the rest "popular") plus nine national dailies (of which four are "quality")—and that does not take into account the American-owned and -edited daily, the *International Herald Tribune*.

Yet oligopoly has been a consistent concern for many years—at least enough to stir repeated inquiries. Royal Commissions were created for this purpose in Britain in 1947–49, 1961–62, and 1974–77; to which must be added an exhaustive three-volume survey of the national newspaper industry published in 1966 by the *Economist* Intelligence Unit. The most recent Royal Commission said: "This reflects an anxiety about the press which has been matched in most other democratic countries in Europe."

But concern has been one thing, action another. Since 1965, newspaper mergers in Britain have been subject to the jurisdiction of the Monopolies and Merger Commission. Seven cases, including the merger of the *Times* with the *Sunday Times*, have been referred to that Commission; all have been approved.[38]

The Royal Commission proposed to deal with this situation

through a series of recommendations aimed, first, at tightening the standards for merger approval; second, at limiting cross-ownership of commercial radio and television stations so as to bar the acquisition of effective control by newspapers; and third, at requiring disclosure of other commercial interests when these are being treated in a publication's news or editorial columns.

The Royal Commission took the view that it would be unwise to preclude altogether the kind of cross-subsidy that can arise from diversified holdings. Both the *Times* and the *Guardian* are supported by such subsidies. The fact is that the economic health of the newspaper industry, with some significant exceptions, is not strong. Newsprint prices have trebled in recent years, and labor represents by far the greatest cost.[39] And so it is natural for management, in the continuing effort to preserve press viability and independence, to look for labor-saving and paper-saving techniques.

4. *Electronic publishing.* Recent advances in computer science and in telecommunications make possible such techniques as electronic text editing and photocomposition. These could return far greater product control to journalists and editors, and make redundant a large proportion of the typesetting and related work force. The labor unions, of course, realize this; and they are currently engaged in negotiations the outcome of which may have a decisive effect on the future of the industry.[40]

If the press succeeds in achieving a satisfactory arrangement, it will find itself for the first time in the electronic production business. The next question will be: Why not go into electronic distribution? Facsimile delivery of the newspaper to the home is still considered to be some years off. But already there is teletext—the provision of previously stored information, on demand, to the home television screen in the form of words and numbers. The British broadcasters have developed a relatively low-capacity system called CEEFAX in the BBC's version, or ORACLE in the IBA's, which provides something of a headline service. The British Post Office is now introducing a much higher-capacity system called Viewdata, which links television receivers through the telephone system to information stored in computers. This system is very well suited, for example, to the presentation of classified advertisements. If only for defensive reasons, the press must take an interest in the Viewdata type of wired teletext: The "quality" press in Britain now gets from 18 to 24 percent of its revenues from classified advertisements, whereas a majority of the revenues of the provincial press comes from this source.[41]

In West Germany and in Britain, the press has stepped forward to claim a right of control over the new technology. The German press wants to run the teletext side of certain pilot projects using broadband cable communications.[42] The British press told the Annan Committee and the Royal Commission that there should be a moratorium on deployment of teletext systems, or, failing that, newspaper publishers should have a prescriptive right to participate in ownership and management of these systems.[43] Both bodies refused the request, and the Royal Commission went so far as to propose that there be no acquisition of control by the press.

This represents, as previously suggested, the debit side of having no regulatory body for the press: There is no one in government to champion its interests in the inevitable inter-industry jockeying for a place in the new electronic technologies and services. This is not to say that the price of having such a champion would be acceptable, far from it. Nor does it suggest that the struggle has been decided. Under ground rules recently developed by the British Post Office, anyone who wishes to be a Viewdata "information provider" may do so. The newspapers could continue to collect classified advertisements, place them in the computer under the appropriate heading, and sell them to Viewdata subscribers who order up that service on their screens.

Furthermore, British Post Office policies will permit any newspaper or other entity that wishes to do so to become not only an Information Provider but a full-fledged Viewdata entrepreneur, leasing telephone lines from the Post Office and hooking up its own computers to serve the public directly.[44] If electronic publishing is to be the wave of the future, there is no technical or legal reason for the press to hang back.

D.   New Technologies and Services

Here we shall look at a small sampling of representative new services, which for our purposes may be defined as recent or currently pending services, based on newly developed technology, and having at least some tendency to confound established distinctions in the communications industry—such as those between point-to-

point and mass media, or between printed and electronic messages. They are the "convergence" services, and their introduction
presents both conceptual and practical difficulties.

In Western Europe considerable debate exists at present about
whether the new services can be provided, by whom, and under
what system of control. The tendency is to argue from analogy to
existing services, each of which operates within its own well-
developed juridical and institutional framework, rather than to examine the new service in its own right. There is nothing new about
that penchant, of course: Radio when first introduced was called a
"wireless telegraph," and that precise terminology can still be
found on today's British license to use a color television set. In
America as well, broadband cable was long regarded for jurisdictional purposes as a branch of the broadcasting industry; and it is
still regulated so as to protect the operations of over-the-air broadcasting. But in Europe the tendency is probably more pronounced,
and it likely has a more severe suppressive effect on the development of new services.

Apart from the provision of video discs and video cassettes,
whose functional resemblance to book and phonograph-record
publishing has allowed them a private-enterprise status, all of the
new communications services in Europe have been claimed as the
province of one or more state enterprises and ministries. We may
consider in turn broadband cable, satellites, broadcasting text (à la
CEEFAX) and telephone text (à la Viewdata).

1. *Broadband cable* transmits intelligence by wire and to that
extent resembles the telephone system. Never mind that its services are only potentially two-way, or that cable has been used
primarily for the transmission of television pictures of a bandwidth
broader than can be carried over conventional telephone wires.
The PTT monopolies have claimed exclusive jurisdiction. In
France, for example, Postes et Télécommunications has built a
cable television system in the city of Rennes but has used it only for
data, facsimile and similar services. No television programs have
yet been carried on this system.[45]

In Britain the Post Office has licensed a number of private cable
television systems, serving in the aggregate about one million subscribers; the Post Office has, however, reserved the right to recap-
ture these systems at any time for its monopoly. In Britain, as in
France, there have been a few state-financed experiments with ad-

vanced cable services; but financial support has been halting and has produced little in the way of firm results.

Because cable systems could deliver either off-the-air or original programming in competition with broadcasting organizations, broadcasters have also intervened negatively. In Britain the Home Office licenses and restricts program carriage by cable systems, whereas in France it is asserted that the radio and television broadcasting entities have participated in cable experiments only to hinder them.

In West Germany, the KtK report recommended further pilot projects with cable systems but left open the question of who would conduct them. This had led to something of a minor donnybrook. In Berlin the city authorities have come up with a plan for an interactive broadband system with very little radio or television programming but a great deal of both "dialogue" and "distribution" services: cultural and consumer news, education, classified information exchange and entertainment. Both the broadcasting organizations and the newspaper publishers have seized on various aspects of these services to claim that they should run all or a significant part of the system. The Berlin authorities have thus far resisted these claims. They have proposed establishing a new public body which would represent not only those two groups but others in society.[46]

It may be that such rivalries have developed more or less cynically to curtail the development of broadband cable services that might compete with those currently offered by established communications industries. What seems certain is that, until jurisdictional stalemates are resolved, cable can have little place in the European communications future.

2. *Communications satellites* are microwave stations in space and would probably be claimed by the PTT monopolies so long as some point-to-point traffic is carried on them. At present, satellites are used by the PTT's, broadcasting organizations and private organizations including press services.[47]

No satellite services have been developed for individual European countries because of their relatively small size. The European Space Agency manages non-broadcasting communications satellites for the region. Furthermore, following the 1977 World Administrative Conference's allocation of frequencies for direct broadcasting satellites, regional planning for that service is now well under way. Under one set of arrangements in which France will participate, each of a group of European countries will have five new channels allocated to it. In preparation for the expanded programming this will require, the Institut National de l'Audiovisuel is currently experimenting with ways to utilize television for public information about the concerns of a wide variety of geographic and interest groups.

There is no disposition to challenge the exclusive state responsibility over satellites. No "open skies" proposal such as that adopted in the United States has been heard. It is not even known whether French, British or German commercial firms have any desire to put up their own satellites. Whatever detriment may arise from the absence of such private competition, the state monopolies will be in a position to generate the internal cross-subsidies needed to serve all elements of the population—a strong consideration for West European governments.

3. *Broadcasting text* uses a blanking interval in the television picture to transmit alphanumeric (words and numbers) information. It can be used for picture-related services, such as the United States' PBS system of captioning for the deaf. In Western Europe, however, a more extensive system has been developed to provide "pages" of information entirely unrelated to the programs being broadcast. Broadcasting organizations have been first in the field, starting with the BBC's CEEFAX system and the IBA's closely comparable ORACLE. As was stated in the German KtK report:

> Since videotext (broadcasting text) is regarded as broadcast according to the definition of the legal term broadcast by the Länder, the broadcasting organizations under public law are responsible for the text contents.[48]

In practice, things have not been quite that simple. In France, the broadcast transmission monopoly TDF has developed its own broadcasting text system, called ANTIOPE. But the PTT monopoly, which has developed a telephone text system called TICTAC, has asserted that there can be no commercial deployment of any species of teletext except under its auspices. Matters are currently at a standstill.[49]

In West Germany, the newspaper publishers' association has draped the label of *Bildschirmzeitung* or "screen newspaper" across both broadcasting and wired systems of teletext, to further its claim to offer these services. Rival claims to supply broadcasting text have been put forward by the two television networks. The struggle centers over who should have primacy in exercising editorial and publishing skills to select and display information of general public interest. For although the data bank is relatively limited, to about 250 "pages," it can be kept up-to-date and could become a competitor to the evening news either on television or in the newspapers.

4. *Telephone text* is both technically and functionally a very different service. It is interactive, in the sense that a subscriber dials the category of information wanted. It is a billable service by virtue of its connection through the telephone. And it provides a virtually unlimited reservoir of retrievable information; the pioneering Viewdata system in the U.K. can already provide more than 70,000 "pages" and this is before its scheduled (winter 1979) full-scale commercial introduction.

Britain again is in the lead, but comparable systems have also been developed in France (TICTAC), West Germany (Bildschirmtext) and Finland (Telset). Marketing efforts are being mounted for other countries including the United States—whose only system thus far has been a New York cable television arrangement serving institutions with information compiled by Reuters.[50]

All of the European systems have been developed by or licensed to a PTT, and there seems to to be no quarrel with such jurisdiction over the service. As the German KtK reported, telephone text may be regarded as an extension of the recorded information service of the Bundespost, even though the legal discussion is "not yet completed."[51] The most significant fact is that the Bundespost and other PTT's will not involve themselves in matters of content. The service is to be operated as a transparent intermediary between Information Providers—who will bear responsibility for the accuracy and inoffensiveness of their own content—and the subscribing public.

This can present certain problems. The 1969 Post Office Act in Britain, for reasons that are not clear, withholds common carrier status from the Post Office. This could mean that, until its status is corrected, the Post Office would be subject to legal liability for errors or other defects in the content of information supplied by third parties. The Carter Committee took a brief look at this question but declined to recommend a statutory change. With commercial trials in prospect, the Post Office took its own initiative and required legal indemnification from each of its Information Providers—leaving editorial responsibility squarely with them.[52] This may serve for the tests but the situation will bear watching.

The British Post Office guidelines for Viewdata make clear that anyone is entitled to be an Information Provider and presumably to use telephone billing services to recover fees from subscribers. (There is no requirement of a charge, of course, and some will prefer to offer free information or advertising through the new medium.) Of even greater potential significance is the announced policy of open entry for would-be telephone text entrepreneurs. Anyone who wants to lease lines from the Post Office and to compete with it may do so, with one important exception. Viewdata has the capacity to provide a private electronic mail facility: one subscriber sending a brief message to the central computer which alerts the recipient to its pendency when he next switches on the service. If this proves attractive to viewers, they will not be inclined to shift to a privately managed telephone text system—because the Post Office has already decided that the electronic mail service falls under its government monopoly.

Leaving that to one side, the manager of Viewdata believes that initially private entry could be fairly widespread. The PTT's may be slow to unravel themselves. In France there is jurisdictional rivalry, as we have seen, and the PTT tariffs for TICTAC are high. A would-be private telephone text operator has the precedent of computer service bureaus, which are allowed to lease lines for data retrieval so long as they do not go into the general message business. Private firms, the manager believes, may be first to go into the telephone text field in a number of European countries.

III
Selected
Policy Issues*

A. Monopoly versus Competition

1. *Telecommunications.* Given the extensive state control over
the operations of the electronic communications industries, it is
not surprising to discover among Western European policymakers
a limited enthusiasm for market competition. In the telephone industry, for example, nothing resembles the American policies of
open entry into satellite markets, competition among carriers for
specialized business services, or provision of terminal equipment
by suppliers other than the telephone company.

European PTT's such as the West German and the British do
allow private installation of some in-house switching systems (PBX)
and facsimile machines. About half of all PBX'es in West Germany

---

* The policy issues selected for analysis in this study correspond in the main to the policy
chapters in the Aspen Institute's major report on U.S. communications policymaking—
Communications for Tomorrow: Policy Perspectives for the 1980s—alongside which it may
profitably be read. There are two exceptions, each deriving from the availability of relevant
information. The present volume devotes extended attention to formal and informal controls
over broadcast programming, because the variety of West European approaches to this
question is well documented and because it offers an array of stimulating contrasts to the
American experience as described in the earlier report by Professor Benno Schmidt. On
the other hand, there is no counterpart in this essay to the appraisal by William Lucas of
the social uses of advanced telecommunications technologies and services. A survey of West
European plans and practices for electronic delivery of health care, education and other social benefits would require, and would doubtless merit, a separate study. To summarize,
this Part III should be read in conjunction with Chapters 3–6 and 8–9 of the earlier Aspen
Institute report.

are supplied in this fashion.[53] The equipment is licensed by the PTT and maintained by it; interface devices are supplied and standards set by the PTT. All these arrangements provide methods of retaining effective control.

The PTT's also lease telephone circuits for *internal* data communications purposes, that is, for transmissions within a single corporation or by a computer service bureau with its customers. The circuits may not be connected to the public telecommunications networks or used for general message traffic.[54] Policing this restriction can involve the PTT in the actual monitoring of data being passed between the computer and the recipient, to assure that it is in fact private traffic. British Post Office representatives confess to some unease with this practice, on the ground of invasion of privacy; but they see no alternative while the restriction persists.

There is a strong tendency to price new services in a way that will protect the rate structure of established services. Telex for example has been a very profitable business service, returning a healthy surplus that supports telephone service and helps keep its prices down. However, in comparison to packet switching, which transmits large volumes of data without routing delays at low per-unit cost, telex is like a stately carriage being overflown by a jet plane. The answer of the European PTT's has been to slow down the plane by attaching heavier rate burdens or service restrictions, thereby allowing the telex "carriage" to maintain its pace and position.

This sort of policy, of course, presents problems of accommodation between Europeans and Americans. The U.S. policy, developed over the past ten years, has been increasingly to favor market competition for electronic point-to-point services in any market where it cannot be shown to produce an unacceptable risk of deterioration of message services of general public interest. While this policy is by no means free from controversy, it has in some instances demonstrably fostered service innovation and the satisfaction of previously unmet customer needs.

There has even been progression in the United States towards a policy whereby only the basic carrier, or facilities owner, would be regulated; those leasing its circuits would be treated as private firms whose dealings with customers would be left unsupervised. This would apply, for example, to a packet switching enterprise, which operates no transmission facilities of its own and therefore could be classified as a "broker" rather than a "carrier." With no

U.S. restrictions on entry into the business, several such "brokers" might in theory approach the British Post Office to do transatlantic business. The European PTT's still regard such activity as the business of the carrier, however, and their monopoly frame of mind would lead them to insist on dealing with just one firm—a clear case of conflict.

The case should not be overdrawn. Strong elements of monopoly still exist in American thinking about electronic point-to-point services, just as some openings for competition appear in the European viewpoint. But because of the need for physical linkages across the ocean, the contrasts in policy that do exist are of more than analytical interest. The Europeans have the capacity to frustrate the trans-border implementation of American policies that impinge on their own, or they may feel pushed reluctantly towards adoption of American views of industrial organization. "I suppose you fellows will keep pressing until we're forced to adjust our entire pricing schedule," is how one senior British Post Office official has put it. There are clear practical necessities for each side to try to understand the other and to come to some tolerable harmonization of structural policies.

When Europeans are drawn to experiment with competitive arrangements, the steps they take can be very tentative. The Carter Commission in Britain suggested some liberalization of restrictions on the competitive supply of telephone terminal equipment, and recommended a limited field trial. It further advised turning the question over to its proposed Council on Post Office and Telecommunications Affairs—in effect, a citizens' advisory group. It is difficult to know what such an amateur body could accomplish across the range of technical and economic questions involved in terminal equipment competition; in the United States it has taken the Federal Communications Commission and the Federal courts nearly ten years to resolve them. It may be, of course, that the British approach would sidestep adversary proceedings, find the underlying issues to be quite manageable, and demonstrate how to settle public questions quickly.

In the meantime, it is worth noting that telephone handsets are sold quite openly by independent retailers in London shops; the British Post Office evidently turns a blind eye to this entrepreneurial incursion into the monopoly it currently claims.

Technical questions, if not economic, tend to dominate the discussion on deployment of new telecommunications devices. Because interconnection is at the heart of any electronic point-to-point system, standardization and compatibility are seen as prerequisites to development of any new part of the system. This has always been the view of Bell System engineers in the United States, but in European PTT's the engineers tend to be in charge of policy rather than just one important voice in its making. Economists and lawyers are not given the same prominence in the policy debate as they are in America. And because decisions are made within the PTT rather than by a neutral body hearing from all interested parties, the voice of technical rationalization tends to be dominant.[55] Again, this primacy can be significant for other communications industries such as cable and broadcasting.

2. *Broadcasting.* Before considering the prospects of competitive challenges to broadcasting by new technologies, it is well to examine the extent of openness that may exist or evolve within the structure of European broadcasting. Competition within the broadcasting monopoly, it will be recalled, has been tried in some countries with varying results. On paper the French and Swedish television systems—two or three networks with separate management—look quite similar, but the coverage of public affairs by the two systems is entirely dissimilar. As one knowledgeable Dutch observer has put it, the Swedish purpose is to inform whereas the French purpose is to lull.[56] Without legislative or other controlling guidelines, a mere change in the administrative structure of French broadcasting has not been enough to introduce genuine liberty of expression. In fact there were no programming policy objectives behind the 1974 French reforms and no real change has taken place.

The Netherlands, of course, has a history of robust broadcast competition among a wide variety of social philosophies and a system of open entry to keep the television screen alive with new ideas as they gather popular support. In practice, however, the admission of TROS and VOO has launched a scramble among almost all programming groups for the lowest common denominator of mass tastes; and the Dutch government is currently considering changes that would restrict future entry to groups representing specific and presently unarticulated points of view within the population.[57]

Fear of lowered programming standards has been a principal reason for West European resistance to commercial broadcasting and for the limitations placed on advertising, where it is permitted at all. Yet, as the British experience has shown, competition from a commercial network can be a force for diversity and expanded viewer choice. There has long been a lively interest in the possibility of commercial broadcasting in West Germany, which has tended since the war to look to Britain for a model. The Federal Constitutional Court in its 1961 decision held that a state-run monopoly was permissible, not that it was mandatory. So far, however, the Länder have not seen fit to authorize commercial stations or a commercial network, despite continuing speculation by journalists that such developments might be forthcoming.

Open entry into both commercial and ideological broadcasting has now arrived in Italy, at the local level, by force of judicial pronouncements and not of government policy. Elsewhere in Europe, the Italian experience tends to be described in terms of civil anarchy. But the Italian Constitutional Court based its judgment on a clause in the Italian Constitution guaranteeing freedom of expression, and there is at least some evidence that the range and social utility of broadcast information have increased as a result of the Court's decision.[58] Similar free-speech clauses are to be found in the written constitutions of France and Germany. Indeed, the recent lower-court decision in France, refusing to honor the statutory public monopoly over broadcasting transmission, expressly relied on such a "First Amendment" clause. One can speculate that the more rigid state broadcasting monopolies may eventually come to be somewhat liberalized by their governments as a safeguard against sweeping judicial decrees.

The most extensive liberalization to be proposed in recent years in Western Europe is that recommended by the Annan Committee in Britain. It looked at alternative ways to structure a "fourth channel" of television and came up with an entirely new device: an Open Broadcasting Authority. Rather than handing control of the channel over to the BBC or to ITV (commercial broadcasting), it would create a Netherlands-type system of access open to all would-be broadcasters, but without advance eligibility requirements of either membership or social purpose. Thus the independent production companies of ITV could present programs, as could the Open University (patrons of higher education on television). But to quote from the Annan Committee report:

Above all, there will be programmes from a variety of independent producers. We attach particular importance to this third category as a

force for diversity and new ideas. . . . We would expect the OBA
(Open Broadcasting Authority), by commissioning from independent
producers, to guarantee a place where new ideas for programming
can flourish. . . . We stress that we see the new Authority as a publisher, which commissions programmes. Its aim should be to encourage productions which say something in new ways; we recommend
accordingly.[59]

This concept of "publishing," of openness to independent
points of view, has potentially revolutionary implications for the
relationship of government to broadcasters and of broadcasters to
the citizenry. Broadcasting in Europe and in America has developed as a paternalistic system, one in which a very few people
choose—within governmentally defined limits—what to say to a
great many people. American broadcasters, for example, are called
"trustees" of the public interest. In Britain itself, the BBC has
been characterized as top-heavy, and a group of BBC producers
proposed that it be broken up into 15 autonomous production centers. The Annan Committee brushed that suggestion aside with the
observation that in a structure like the BBC there would inevitably
be a pull towards the center.[60] That centrifugal system would have
to contend, if the OBA idea were adopted, with a rival scheme
where power would pass to program-makers rather than network
administrators.

We shall consider further the implications of this arrangement
for programming in the next Section on "Programming Pluralism
and Content Controls."

Translating the Annan concepts into economic and political reality has proved to be a difficult task. Programming costs for the
fourth channel are estimated at between 25 and 40 million pounds
a year. Presumably such sums could be readily obtained from the
advertising market, but there are two difficulties. First, a good deal
of the revenues would be withdrawn from provincial and national
newspapers; the chairmen of the Broadcasting and Press Commissions evidently reached an agreement not to risk such injury to the
press. Second, dependence upon advertising would give a great
advantage to the existing ITV production companies, which would
tend to shoulder out the independent producers and turn an
"open" network into a commercial one. This the Annan Committee
resolved to prevent.

The committee's solution was to propose financing from (1)
sponsored programs, akin to those seen on American public televi-

sion; (2) charitable grants, such as those that launched the U.S. Children's Television Workshop; and (3) advertising in blocs, which would mean no commercial purchase of particular programs and would bring in far less revenue. The Annan Committee was unsure whether these sources, taken together, would produce enough finance. A majority was therefore willing to look to government grants to fill in the gap—despite the fully acknowledged risk of inviting governmental intervention into programming. The minority proposed the equally risk-fraught expedient of letting the ITV production companies sell spot advertising. In the end, the Committee was unable to agree on either of these matters, although resolution of the financing question is an indispensable prerequisite to achieving a genuinely open channel.[61]

Finance, along with political caution, also affected the manner of presentation of the proposal to government. Because of the economic climate of the moment, the Committee reported, the Open Broadcasting Authority should be established only when the nation's economy would permit the kind of service being proposed. "This may not be until the 1980's," the Committee judged.[62] It knew, of course, that the ITV companies had wanted control over the whole channel and would be likely to mount a forceful lobby for that position; allowing the Home Secretary to take refuge in the state of the general economy might blunt the assault and also allow time for the new idea of open broadcasting to gain acceptance.

The British Government has chosen to deal with the issue directly through the issuance of a White Paper. A definite position may have to await the outcome of the next Parliamentary election, but it seems likely that Britain will either accept or reject the Open Broadcasting Authority before the end of 1979.* Its decision could influence attitudes throughout Western Europe, not only to broadcasting but also to alternative means of program origination and distribution, such as cable.

3. *Broadband cable.* If broadcasting could be structured to offer an outlet for creative diversity, much of the social attrac-

---

* After completion of this manuscript, in the summer of 1978, the Labour Government at length produced the long-awaited White Paper. This document supported the essentials of the "open channel" idea, without however resolving the difficult problems of financing such a venture. The White Paper also advanced various proposals for the future governance of the BBC, which that institution has taken as a serious challenge to its future autonomy. It remains likely that a definitive British policy in all these matters will emerge only in the aftermath of the next general election.

tiveness of cable and of other new technologies could be undercut. Broadcasting is generally seen in Western Europe as the premier electronic media service because it is the only one that speaks to a mass audience. It links an otherwise fragmenting society with common topics and a sense of shared culture. So said the Annan Committee, adding that no other communications service performs this function.[63]

But multi-channel cable could provide access to all sorts of social, cultural and political voices—something that broadcasting as a mass service has not done. The objective has seemed sound to many Americans, but not to the Annan Committee. Access, in its view, implies "a claim to make others listen"; if access were imposed, the television screen "would have to become an aerial Hyde Park corner."[64] The short answer would seem to be that no one need go to or stay in Hyde Park corner, whether on the ground or on the air. Indeed, the only ostensible reason that broadcasting is not organized along open-access lines (following its predecessor wired-telegraph service) is the scarcity of available frequencies. Since cable is virtually unaffected by this limitation, it would seem well equipped to meet social purposes that broadcasting has not met.

But Europeans tend not to see things that way. Like teletext, videorecorders, cassettes and discs, cable is viewed as a potential fragmenter of audiences for mass programs. When it comes to pay programming on cable, which is probably essential to financing a full range of the services that could make use of cable's broad bandwidth, the response can be emphatically negative. Thus again, the Annan Committee characterized pay cable as "a ravenous parasite," feeding on live sports and feature films.[65] The Committee did not consider how the authorization of such a service— which it refused to endorse— might actually help the film industry in Britain, where theater admissions have declined by 90 percent over the past 15 years and where there is no longer any domestic production to speak of.

The truth seems to be that the Annan Committee was determined to protect programming opportunities for its fourth channel. It recognized that the mass audience is already crumbling because of changes in work shifts and the acquisition of more than one television receiver per family. People therefore want a greater variety of programming choices. But the way to deal with this changed consumption preference is to ladle out a fourth and then a fifth channel, in an orderly fashion.[66]

The disorderliness of cable—its capacity to provide an unpredictable variety of services that could disrupt established patterns—seems behind much of the West European disinclination to foster its growth. There seems also to be an acceptance of what may be called the myth of the finite programming pie—the notion that a nation's creative resources are limited and if they are drawn to cable they will be lost to broadcasting. If it is difficult to square such a concept with the vitality of London's West End theater district, it is nonetheless important to recognize the hold of this view on current broadcasting and cable policy.

Cable is found in such places as the Low Countries where the interest in imported programming outweighs concern about domestic broadcasts. Fifty percent of Dutch homes, for example, have a cable connection. They get German stations and Flemish broadcasts from Belgium. In Belgium itself, cable is used to bring in French, Dutch and even British broadcasts. New construction is currently underway: Cable systems covering entire cities are now being built in Amsterdam, The Hague and Utrecht. It is quite conceivable that the region could become like the Canadian border with the United States, heavily cabled but with little in the way of access programming or other services beyond over-the-air broadcast relay. Yet even in a small country like the Netherlands, with its flat topography, the government has ruled out the idea of a nationwide cable network.[67]

In the major West European countries, cable development is in an arrested state. In France a recent decree established a government commission to monitor technical standards adopted by the PTT and by TDF (the broadcast transmission monopoly). It defined signal carriage on cable so as to exclude both original programming, including pay cable, and community services.[68] To veterans of the struggle to promote French cable, this represented another policy freeze. Five years earlier there had been a flurry of interest when the government announced seven cable experiments. Six never became operational and the seventh, at Grenoble, was closed in 1976 when the government withdrew from further funding.

In West Germany the KtK said it found no evidence of pronounced demand for cable services and reported that inter-active or two-way cable would be too expensive to warrant the construction of a nationwide network. It too recommended a series of pilot projects, such as those in France and England which have proved to be temporizing devices.

The German and the British approaches to cable development show a marked similarity. Both recognize, as they must, that the audience-fractionating potential of video cassettes and discs is beyond their control. These, according to the KtK report, are "not covered by the legal term broadcast. Therefore their production and sale are not subject to any restriction, but determined by the law of supply and demand."[69] And the Annan Committee conceded that video disc pricing could precipitate a breakthrough of these new devices into the mass market, thereby upsetting current projections and policy. But neither committee felt disposed by these concessions to consider letting cable operate in a free-enterprise environment. Since its growth could be controlled, it would be.

There is also an inclination to put a technical hold on deployment of cable. The Annan Committee advised waiting for the evolution of a single, standardized, broadband system to carry both switched and distributed traffic. This would allow time for waveguides and optical fibers to be integrated into the system. Similarly, the KtK proposed that its pilot projects serve as a means of designing full compatibility into future, more extensive systems.[70]

There is, finally, a common appreciation of the financial picture. The KtK looked at the current investments of the Bundespost (the German PTT), which would bear the cost of installing a broadband cable infrastructure, and noted that they already amount to one-fifth of the investment in tangible assets of all German industry.[71] By implication, any added expenditure for new systems would have to be weighed against the existing burden. In Britain, where the Annan Committee likewise looked to the Post Office for broadband investment, the cost of building a national cable system with local components was put at 1 billion pounds. This would be beyond budgetary reach until the 1990s, the Committee judged, by which time costs might be down.

The net effect of all this is to treat cable as a starveling, with no significant government support or encouragement. Here and there will be found some grants for local experiments but not in a fashion calculated to appeal to the public. The whole question of competition to the broadcasting system will be put off for 15 years, assuming that video discs and other free-market technologies, not now developed, remain in abeyance commercially. That will provide time for technical and financial uncertainties to be reduced; and it will also mean that some other government, some other advisory group, will have to deal with the problem.

There is ground for questioning many of the assumptions adopted by West European policy planners. Demand for new, presently unknown services may be inchoate but it is not impervious to stimulation. A global financing burden may be too large for governments but that need not rule out private entrepreneurs operating in, and subject to the disciplines of, the capital markets. Technical prevision may be imperfect but standards can be designed flexibly to adapt to future evolutions. Above all, there is no reason to believe that today's uncertainties are any greater than will be those of tomorrow.

But to say all this simply highlights the essentially political nature of the choices being made in Western Europe with respect to deployment of the new, multi-purpose communication technologies and services. The decision for monopoly or competition, or some variation of either, represents at base a value choice of some importance. This may become clearer from our consideration of the topic in the next Section.

B. Programming Pluralism and Content Controls

A monopoly or oligopoly structure in broadcasting concentrates control over programming. This turns the networks into arbiters of mass taste in entertainment and confers on them a power over social and political expression that governments have come to fear. One way of diluting that power would be to expand the number and variety of voices capable of expressing themselves either within the broadcasting medium or via competitive technologies. West European governments have, by and large, chosen not to take that route but have instead imposed a variety of content controls or limitations on the freedom of expression of the broadcasting monopolies.

This is a political choice with significant political repercussions. The decision in its starkest form is one between a kind of centrally directed culture, with its 1984 overtones of groupthink, and the cultural diversity that could be attained through presently available technologies as a reflection and promotion of a pluralistic society. It is a choice that could be made in favor of John Stuart Mill's marketplace of ideas, which cannot readily operate if programming choices are centrally determined.

1. *Pluralism today.*   There is in fact some small but growing support for a liberalizing policy direction. As put by media scholar and former BBC editor Anthony Smith:

> Only in very recent years has any important debate developed, still at the radical fringe of the broadcasting world, about the possibility that television organizations could be provided with a publishing function separated from a control function: this would mean that writers, producers, pressure groups, politicians, could somehow be enabled to use the medium in their own names, unmediated by members of the tiny professional elite.[72]

For Americans accustomed to struggling for a television glimpse of even the major audience events, such as the Olympic games or the political conventions or the Bicentennial celebrations, and finding themselves blocked by the constant and gratuitous intercession of professional mediators, this vision seems promising.

It is one that was shared, at least to a degree, by the Annan Committee. That group was unwilling to concede that the power of British broadcasting authorities should be curbed or shared internally with their producers: "We have not uncovered any evidence of concentrations of power which are deliberately perverting the use of the frequencies to their own ends." But the Committee did think that power should be used to open up the system, to admit diversity:

> It should be the BBC's aim to ensure that many different views are heard; and, if their own producers echo each other, to commission work from independent producers.. . . . In other words, there should be a slight shift in emphasis from the BBC's role as the author of the material it broadcasts towards its role as a publisher and programme maker. But this will carry with it an obligation to search for writers and producers who see the world from different stand-points and that programmes are not made to reflect the clichés of the intelligentsia.[73]

The trouble with this exhortation is that it is very difficult to realize in practice. Broadcasting organizations want to give program-making opportunities to their own producers, technicians and camera crews. They like to know what they are getting in for, which makes them leery of independent points of view. Documentary production companies that do place their work on the BBC find it more difficult to gain access now than they did five or ten years ago. And the going is likely to get tougher as labor unions increasingly resist freelance entrée. The head of the major craft union in Britain has stated that even if the Open Broadcasting Authority is implemented, he will act to restrict programming by independent sources to no more than 25 percent of the total and will scrutinize these productions to weed out any that are made by subsidiaries of large, multinational corporations.[74]

The wave of protectionist sentiment is not limited to unions and their longtime members. It extends to freelance professionals as well, a growing number of whom have succumbed to the lure of assured employment and to pensions and other benefits. When television broadcasting was started in West Germany, more producers were at work as independents than in the employ of the stations. The freelancers had no fringe benefits but they made more money and they had greater freedom. The recessions of the 1960s and 1970s changed their outlook and most of the independent producers have now become employees.[75] As one German observer has put it, there is a practical conflict between two clauses in the German Federal Constitution, one guaranteeing freedom of expression and the other assuring security of employment; in this particular field, freedom of expression has lost out.[76]

Resort to other technologies such as broadband cable might provide a solution by furnishing enough new outlets for expression so that employment security would become less pressing. There has in fact been some small service paid to the concept of access programming that this would entail. In Britain, the cable experiments in Swindon and Milton Keynes include provisions for access; and in West Germany, the KtK has recommended that the long-term legal framework for cable provide not only for access but also for a separation between control over distribution and control over programming.

Yet in neither country, as we have seen, is cable growth being promoted. The KtK instead proposed that priority be given to expansion of conventional telephone service, as a way of supporting the values of self-realization and community—important values, to be sure, but very much the values that cable enthusiasts claim for their medium. And the Annan Committee expressed considerable distaste for the whole concept of access, "a claim to make others listen"—which is surely the province of a ringing telephone.

It is hard to escape the conclusion that pluralistic programming—always outside of the Netherlands, and leaving aside the special situation of Italy—is an ideal to be saluted but not implemented. To understand this, it is helpful to examine the reasons for resisting an open system and for imposing instead the kinds of content controls we shall consider shortly.

2. *Restrictionist impulses.* One reason, common to both North America and Western Europe, is a concern that broadcasting in general and television in particular can play the role of a Pied Piper, exercising undue influence in setting the agenda of social discussion. There is not a great deal of evidence to support this theory, and many analysts of the medium have come to the view that it is ill-founded. Yet the notion of television power is widely, if uncritically, accepted, which means that policy planners must come to terms with it. Even so, the risk of undue influence could be dissipated by the simple expedient of opening up expression to a multitude of tongues, as has happened in the Netherlands.

But the second and probably weightier reason for restrictionist attitudes, which is not so often heard in North America, is impervious to this type of remedy. It is the fear of political usurpation, the concern that parliaments and governments will not lead but be pushed into decisions by the mobilized force of popular opinion. Until quite recently, in Britain there could be no broadcast treatment of issues pending in Parliament in the fortnight preceding the debate. That restriction has now been lifted, but the policy continues in the form of wary surveillance of the coverage of current affairs. Even talk shows and televised forums are suspect, because they might be the occasion for broadcasters rather than politicians to bring the relevant parties and arguments together for a resolution.[77]

It is difficult to overstate the importance or the pervasiveness of this attitude. To be sure it is reminiscent of postures adopted by Anthony Wedgwood-Benn in Britain and Spiro Agnew in the United States, attacking broadcast commentators as a tiny, unelected and elitist conspiracy. But whereas Agnew's speeches have been thought to represent a minority view among American politicians, in Western Europe this point of view—or variations on it—apparently is held by a majority of at least the politicians currently in positions of authority. To them, it evidently seems essential to contain what Anthony Smith has sardonically called "the dangerous power of arbitrage" held by broadcasters. And that danger would present itself whether the organization intruding on political prerogatives were a public monopoly or a multitude of private programming groups. Because the monopoly is regarded as easier to control, West European governments have exhibited a preference for confining editorial responsibilities to it.

3. *Formal controls.* The principal controls imposed on the content of European broadcasting are similar to those adopted in the United States: fairness in treatment of controversial issues, and equal opportunity for expression of partisan political viewpoints.

(a) "FAIRNESS." This is usually expressed in Europe in terms of a requirement that programming be balanced, objective and impartial. (In Sweden, the balance between opinions and interests is judged over a whole range of output rather than within a single program;[78] not so in most other European countries.) The responsibility to adhere to fair programming standards is laid on the broadcasting authorities, with governments exercising a *post hoc* review. In Sweden, for example, the Radio Council—whose seven members are appointed by the Government—examines previously broadcast programs either on its own initiative or in response to complaints filed with it. The Council has been very supportive in its judgments of positions taken by Sveriges Radio.[79] Indeed, nowhere in Western Europe is there evidence of heavy-handed official enforcement of the balance or objectivity regulations.

Nonetheless, resistance to these controls exists among thoughtful and creative people in television, just as in the United States. Some say that impartiality is an unattainable and even a disturbing goal. Jonathan Dimbleby, editor and correspondent of the excellent documentary program *This Week,* asks what would happen if one were obliged to balance pro-slavery and anti-slavery views on the same show. Others have abandoned the goal of balance. In Swedish broadcasting, the younger announcers were allowed, in the heady atmosphere of the late 1960s, to adopt a high degree of subjectivity in their treatment of current affairs; and, although it is receding, much of this insistence on personal statement can still be heard. In West Germany, similarly, if the complaints of the "Establishment" are to be credited, television news on a number of stations has a sermonizing quality that appears aimed at indoctrination rather than information.

There is, behind these tensions, a seldom-acknowledged tendency towards balance on a broader scale. The European press barons who have wielded the greatest popular influence are often conservative and even extremely right wing. It is not too surprising that liberals and socialists should seek to make television their forum of influence and to rebel against content controls that are not imposed on their ideological opposites in the print medium.[80]

In simplistic terms, however, the defenders of television content controls say they are necessary to constrain the ideological assertiveness of the young people who have taken up important positions in broadcasting. And the questions of people like Dimbleby are met by the exemption of certain subjects from the requirement of balanced treatment. In Britain, the insurrectionist activities of the IRA and the racial exclusivity of apartheid have been placed outside the pale of impartial discussion; both are seen as attacking the fundamental order of constitutional government and civilized social relations, and neither is to be accorded objective treatment.[81] Similarly in Sweden—by express agreement rather than informal understanding, as in Britain—Sveriges Radio is not to remain neutral in the struggle between democracy and dictatorship. "The corporation shall, in its programmes, defend the fundamental democratic values."[82] While probably alleviating strains that would otherwise arise from the balance requirement, these exemptions come close to an official doctrine that could have a blinkering effect on examination of the causes of resistance to the established order.

Interestingly, editorializing on West European television is generally prohibited. The BBC license, for example, incorporates a Prescribing Memorandum that forbids the expression of opinion on current affairs or on matters of public interest. To the extent that this restraint arises from the public financing of the BBC, it could be understood as a safeguard against the reality or appearance of government propaganda. But editorializing is not to be found on independent television either, and West Europeans generally appear unresponsive to the suggestion that the licensing of commercial broadcasting would open up freedom for the expression of editorial opinion. Again, the power of merchant princes seems more to be feared than the power of governments.

The ban on editorializing could help explain the movement of some television journalists toward "subjectivity," but either the relationship has not been perceived or lifting the ban seems too high a price to pay for the possible eradication of personal slants on the news. Editorials are a formal expression by station management and therefore weightier than the statements of individual correspondents. It is again the fear of usurpation of parliamentary prerogatives that lies behind the prohibition.

(b) "EQUAL TIME." As for equal political opportunity, most broadcasting organizations in Western Europe have a statutory or contractual obligation to cover the sessions of parliament. In the French Chambre des Députés, for example, two cameras are permanently affixed to the balcony and duly record all formal speeches. The West German Bundestag has a similar arrangement, and it can be a valuable resource for documentary film-makers; a recent biography of Chancellor Helmut Schmidt drew heavily on this archival material. It is extremely rare, however, for anything but brief excerpts to appear on home television screens. Interviews outside the chamber are preferred.

There are some exceptions to this generalization. In the Netherlands, live coverage has been given to debates on issues of major concern, such as Prince Bernhard's involvement with Lockheed, and quick "flashes" to other lively debates may take place at any time while Parliament is in session.[83] In Britain the BBC has recently started up live radio coverage of afternoon sessions centering on the Question Period. But neither arrangement conveys a sense of the staple business of the legislature, neither shows its committees or caucuses at work, and neither is regularly scheduled for prime-time audiences.

This seems an unfortunate underutilization of an opportunity that is not yet available in the United States, where Congress has thus far withheld agreement to be televised regularly. In all the democratic countries, the tendency over the past 40 to 50 years has been for legislatures to cede authority to the executive. Broadcasting has accelerated that trend. A president or prime minister can commandeer attention to his proposals through radio and television, whereas opposition leaders typically lack the capacity to suggest the full range of alternative options that merit consideration. It has been said that parliamentary inefficiency is the surest safeguard of liberty because it slows down action on ill-considered proposals. But a public that does not see its parliament in action will not appreciate that fact; it forgets the "efficiency" of Hitler's Reichstag and berates the U.S. Congress for its "inefficient" delay of action on the Carter Administration's hastily drafted energy legislation.

Periodic full coverage of parliamentary sessions, perhaps along the lines proposed some years ago by the Twentieth Century Fund, could go far toward reversing this imbalance of public appreciation for the workings of its democracy. Four evenings a year on issues of major importance, such as defense and tax reform and energy and trade, could reinforce rather than usurp parliamentary prerogatives. If only one or two Western European broadcasting organizations were to adopt this proposal, with the necessary cooperation of political leaders, they could serve as a highly valuable test-bed for the reestablishment in an electronic age of Montesquieu's system of checks and balances. [84]

As it is, the principal vehicle for partisan television expression is the institution of the Party Political Broadcast. In Britain, this takes its shape from a 1947 Aide Memoire and is currently administered by a semiformal committee of the parties. In the periods preceding elections, and also periodically throughout the year, each of the parties is allocated time proportional to its electoral strength for the transmission of any message through any spokesman and with any visual and audio material it chooses. [85] In the Netherlands, ten minutes is provided in rotation to each party every Wednesday while Parliament sits. There are 15 parties, only four of which are sizeable; the rest have only one or two seats, but nevertheless each gets its ten minutes. [86] If each party accepts the offer, consequently, the assiduously attentive Dutch viewer will get to see his own favorite party perhaps three times a year.

These broadcasts cannot be very lively or even informative. Some suggestions have been made that they be abolished in favor of interview programs, or confined to the period immediately before an election. But the politicians evidently lay great store by them, and they are unlikely to be given up.

Interviews with the prime minister (or other leading ministers) are naturally prized; in the Netherlands they take place weekly. A right of reply may be invoked by opposing parties in most West European countries, if obvious partisan advantage is taken of such occasions. [87] The chief of state, however, even when democratically elected like the French President, is not subject to a claim of equal time. Thus M. Giscard d'Estaing was able to commandeer French television before the 1978 legislative elections to urge "the good choice" on his fellow citizens; nobody was heard to object.

More controversial is the right reserved by the British Government in the BBC license to let any Minister require announcements on any subject to be made at a time of his choosing. The antidote to the overreaching that this would seem to encourage is the right of the BBC to state that the announcement is at the Minister's request—a kind of implied "equal opportunity" that serves as a deterrent to all but carefully considered or innocuous uses.[88]

(c) INOFFENSIVENESS. In addition to the "equal time" and "fairness" sorts of controls, there are also more general requirements of inoffensiveness. In American terms, these address the "sex and violence" constellation of issues. In Britain, for example, the broadcasters are obliged to present programs that, so far as possible, do not offend against good taste or decency, are not likely to encourage crime or disorder, and are not offensive to public feeling.

Despite the generality and vagueness of these terms, and the consequent risk that they might be used to curtail unduly the freedom of broadcast expression, the West Europeans seem to treat this whole area of concern in a more mature fashion than the Americans. In France, there is a simple "rectangle blanche" in the corner of the screen for any program that might startle tender sensibilities. And in Britain, despite a determined and well-publicized campaign by Mrs. Mary Whitehouse against any form of expression smacking of moral decay, the Annan Committee was able to treat this issue with a sanity and civilizing judgment that commend themselves to future inquirers. There is, it said in its report, a dynamic and inescapable tension between creative freedom and the sensitivities of the audience. The responsibility for harmonizing this tension must be left with producers and their supervisors. Popular critics of sex, violence and other distressing portrayals must realize that they cannot reduce the tension to simplistic formulas. And the people who are vocal about those shows should perhaps recognize that they have turned a blind eye toward the glorification of base acquisitive instincts that lies just beneath the surface of the very popular give-away shows.[89]

(d) PRIVATE REMEDIES. One last set of formal controls is found in some West European countries. They govern the redress of injury to persons adversely affected by a broadcast misstatement or misrepresentation. In the Netherlands, there is a straightforward and statutory right of reply, or rectification, on radio or television. The Commissioner for Broadcasting, a subordinate of the Minister of Culture, conducts an inquiry and determines whether an injury has been done. If so, he applies to the Amsterdam District Court for an order. The remedy is swift and effective, and the injured party is not required to give up civil or criminal rights of action.[90]

In Britain, matters are not quite so straightforward. Complaints are heard by the broadcasting authorities themselves, which presents at least the appearance of a conflict of interest. Complainants have also been required to waive their right to sue in the courts for defamation, invasion of privacy or comparable legal redress. The Annan Committee considered this unsatisfactory and proposed a unitary and independent Program Complaints Commission, which would use quasi-judicial procedures to determine the facts and fashion an appropriate remedy. The Commission could, for example, order a broadcast apology. The Annan report also expressed unease about the present waiver of legal rights and suggested that its abandonment be considered before the Complaints Commission is established. This aspect of the Annan report has been generally well received.[91]

4. *Informal constraints:* (a) RESERVE POWERS.   But this enumeration of formal controls over broadcasting content does not begin to measure the extent of intrusion by governments and social groups into programming practices. What is visible and hence subject to public reckoning is in some ways and in some places far less significant than the invisible constraints under which broadcasters labor. This is particularly so in Britain, whose broadcasting structure has long provided a model for free and independent expression. Yet the BBC's Broadcasting House also provided the physical model for George Orwell's Ministry of Truth. And most people do not know that the BBC's license reserves sweepingly authoritarian powers over its operation to the relevant minister, now the Home Secretary. Under clause 13(4) of the license, the Secretary may "from time to time by notice in writing require the Corporation to refrain at any specified time or at all times from sending any matter or matter of any class specified in such notice." And under clause 19(1), the Home Secretary may commandeer the whole apparatus of broadcasting and revoke the BBC's license without recourse to Parliament.[92]

On their face, these are totalitarian provisions of the kind one might expect to find in the Soviet Union or in Nazi Germany. They are genuinely astonishing when found in Britain. To be sure, the "reserve powers" have never been invoked and it is unlikely that they ever will be. But it does not take too much imagination to appreciate the inhibiting effect that the mere existence of such powers is likely to have on senior BBC management. At least one person of experience, Anthony Smith, has recounted how the repression actually operates at the program-making level. If a program on Northern Ireland is to be made, Smith relates, or a producer wishes to interview a Scotland Yard official, a body of self-denying precedent built up within the BBC avoids offending government policy. Indeed, there is no need for formal government intervention in any programming sphere, because the BBC itself has anticipated sensitivities and moved to protect them. Formally, the BBC stands up for its program-makers against any government criticism. But within its own walls there is cast a pall of self-restriction all the more devastating for being hidden from the public. The process is not really one of censorship; Smith describes it rather as a continuous negotiation into or out of sensitive and taboo areas. Still, it is a long way from the high ground of freedom and independence on which the public has largely placed the BBC.

(b) SOCIAL PRESSURES. Taboos figure in Swedish programming also, as we have seen, despite the far-reaching provisions of the Swedish Freedom of Information Act. Once again the appearance differs from the reality. On paper, as one perhaps envious German broadcaster has put it, Sweden seems to have given its programmers "more liberty than they can use." But in practice the popular movements, whose dominance of the broadcasting system is an outgrowth of official policy, exercise a conservative influence that blocks political satire and creates restrictions around the treatment of religion, alcohol and the laboring class. This is not to say that these taboos are inappropriate to Swedish society, merely that they contradict the claim of unfettered liberty of expression voiced by Swedish spokesmen like Olof Palme.

(c) POLITICAL POLARIZATION. In France, and in Italy before the recent court decisions, Latin journalistic tradition has tended to override the Anglo-Saxon ideal of objectivity. The Manichean view of society that has prevailed in the Latin countries nourishes a dichotomy of "us" versus "them," of the government in power versus the opposition. This spirit of political polarization is incompatible with the objectives of balance or impartiality.[93] It also makes the treatment of news and public affairs an exercise in spokesmanship for the government, and it makes the whole broadcasting enterprise susceptible to a broad ideological shift if the opposition attains power. Now that France and Italy have entered an era in which each must contemplate Communist assumption of a share of power, the strains are bound to be extensive. In Italy at least the court decisions have paved the way to a sharing of power, by mandating that the parliamentary parties be represented in the governing structure of RAI in accordance with their electoral strengths. The resulting confusion could result in the program producers gaining a greater degree of autonomy. In France, by contrast, where nothing has occurred to dilute the polarization of political perspective, long-term prospects for free or independent expression remain hazardous.

(d) PARTISAN APPOINTMENTS.   Another device for undermining the independence of broadcasting is the *proporz* system of political appointment of management and creative staff.[94] In West Germany today, even the editor of a program is now usually backed up by a deputy who can be said to represent the other major party. This occurs because the two largest German parties think they are diametrically opposed on all important social issues, and neither can afford to risk letting the other gain control of the powerful levers of broadcasting. Also, there is a view that the parties are older than their government or the constitution and are therefore the real repositories of legitimacy in German society. Certainly, the parties are apt to be more broadly representative of that society than particular interest groups, some of which have sought a right of appointment—the Farmers' Association to name the agricultural correspondent and the trade unions, the labor correspondent.

But even as it is, the pressure on television journalists and management must be immense to toe an approved party line or to block someone else from doing so. Remarkably, it is claimed that allegiance grows not to the nominating party but to the broadcasting organization itself as an independent entity. Some German broadcasters even insist that greater freedom of expression exists for a journalist in broadcasting than for one on newspapers.[95] But the struggle to calm the political seas must cost heavily both in time and in distraction; and if the *proporz* system failed to achieve its political ends, it would presumably be abandoned.

5. *Pluralism revisited.*   To show that West European broadcasting need not succumb to such political preoccupation, and to point up again the interrelationship between programming pluralism and content controls, we may look at the current situation in the Netherlands. Balance there is built into the system, through the interplay of the various affiliation groups. No "fair-

ness" requirement is imposed on any program makers. They are expected to be advocates for their own points of view. In order to be credible and to gain adherents, they have to avoid obvious bias; but there is no legal requirement that they do so. The pluralism of views obtainable on the two Dutch channels provides the check on excessive zeal elsewhere attempted through content regulation or political intimidation.

By law, the organizations entitled to transmission time are responsible for the contents of what they broadcast. The obligations they must meet are stated in very general terms, without regard to "fairness": They are expected to respect the security of the State, public order and morality. If these standards are thought to have been breached, the Minister of Culture will consult a statutory Broadcasting Council and may censure the offending organization, debar it from broadcasting for a specified period or withdraw all or part of its share of license-fee revenues.[96]

To show how this statute is enforced, in 1972 VPRO was censured for a television show in which the Queen was impersonated. On appeal to the Council of State, the censure was overturned. And the Minister of Culture has since proposed abolishing the section of the law in question, reserving disciplinary authority only for cases in which a broadcasting organization has been convicted by a court of law.[97]

The pluralistic Dutch system runs into some difficulties in meeting other broadcasting objectives. Each programming entity is currently required to present a comprehensive schedule with cultural, information, educational and entertainment elements "in reasonable proportion." This is difficult to do when the maximum allocation is eight hours and 20 minutes per week. Long documentaries and series programming tend to be excluded. Moreover, the available public and commercial financing is broken up into fairly small packages by the time it is shared among all eight eligible organizations. Since they do not go in for co-productions with each other, large-scale dramatic or other productions are rare.[98]

On the other hand, the system is well suited to the freelance producer. If turned down by one organization, he can turn to several others. Each has a small enough staff to assure his program proposal a full hearing. And if the result of pressures on the system is to encourage a philosophy of "small is beautiful," it is by no means clear that the audience suffers.

In Italy as well, a pluralistic system is being induced or at least attempted by virtue of court decree. Local broadcasting groups (and cable entrepreneurs) enjoy freedom of entry, and no law restricts the programs they can present. Within the RAI itself, provision has been made for access to the government-controlled network. A Parliamentary Commission of 40 members, with proportional representation from the various parties, examines and approves access applications. It is too early to know how well or fully this pluralistic departure for the RAI will be carried out, but already there is at least formal recognition of the liberty of expression that should go with it. Editors of news programs have been given an autonomous status by legislation—making them in theory just like editors of newspapers.

The impetus behind the fourth-channel proposal of the Annan Committee in Britain was similarly to move towards a more pluralistic system. "The greatest temptation in British television in the next fifteen years," the Committee foretold, "will be to continue the present duopoly of BBC and IBA." This approach would consume huge resources and lead to "routines and standardization of methods." The Committee saw the fourth channel as a "challenge to broadcasters." And so it proposed the Open Broadcasting Authority.[99]

The OBA was not to have the same obligations regarding programming as those imposed on its predecessor authorities. It would not be required to schedule a balanced evening with news, sport, entertainment and the like. It would be a publisher and look to its programming "authors" to assume responsibility for content. Although like book publishers it would be subject to such laws as libel and obscenity, it would escape the obligation to balance the presentation of any given program. As with Sveriges Radio in Sweden, the OBA could attain an overall balance of its programs over time. If its programming were consistently slanted, Parliament could be expected to take it out of business. Studied indifference to prevailing tastes and mores would likewise get it into trouble. But the relaxation of the content-controls straitjacket, together with the openness of the OBA to independent producers, could be expected to develop programming not seen and perhaps not acceptable on the first three channels.[100]

There is some hesitancy and some ambiguity in the Committee's description of its proposed departure. Just how would the remaining content controls be administered? Precisely when would liability arise, either administratively or judicially? On these matters the report is too vague to permit business planning. Why did not the Committee opt squarely for the Dutch formulation, which places all responsibility for programming content on the producing organization? Why not treat the OBA as essentially a common carrier? The answer seems to be that this would involve too large a step away from familiar terrain, and the Committee above all wanted not to scare away the intended government readers of its report.

But this merely serves to underline that the dominant state of affairs in Western Europe is oligopoly control of a broadcasting system that is subject to interventionist pressure from governments, political parties and leading social groups. The countervailing movement—towards pluralistic programming opportunities and the dissolution of content controls—is established only in the Netherlands and is struggling for a foothold in Italy and Britain. There is too much concern over broadcasting's influence, and over its capacity to usurp parliamentary prerogatives, for governments to let loose and allow it to become a medium of genuine free expression.

But if organized broadcasting is thought to have such numbing power that it requires political restraint, what of unorganized broadcasting and its potential for participatory democracy? We turn to personalized communications and the special phenomenon of Citizens' Band radio, as an instance of the growing body of alternative consumer choices that may ultimately unravel the pattern of structural and content controls imposed on the present generation of communications services.

C. Fragmentation of the Channels of Discourse

1. *Mobile and personalized communications.* Huey Long, the populist governor of Louisiana, was fond of declaiming: "Every man a King!" Today the cry might be, "Every man a broadcaster." That is the thrust of what has come to be called personalized communications, which involve the use of the airwaves by individuals reaching out to other individuals, known or unknown, without let or hindrance by the established broadcasting institutions. In North America and Australia this form of communication has captured the popular fancy, especially in its Citizens' Band manifestation; during the 1976 U.S. election campaign, the then First Lady Betty Ford made headlines when she picked up a CB transmitter in

Texas and identified herself as "First Momma." The protocols of use of personalized communications make it a democratic form of discourse, in marked contrast to the paternalistic mold in which organized broadcasting has largely developed.

Another important point of distinction is that personalized communications move with the individual who is sending or receiving messages. He or she carries the transceiver in his car, his boat, his briefcase or even on his person. Since these mobile communications must be transmitted over the air, they make a claim on the available radio spectrum, and if they are to grow, some other service must make room. The largest civil user of the spectrum is conventional broadcasting, and part of the (largely undeclared) attraction of cable to American policymakers has been its potential for delivering broadcast signals over shielded transmission paths which would open the way for expansion of mobile and personalized services.

This attraction has registered very little in Western Europe. As the Annan Committee stated flatly, past policy has been opposed to using wire or cable as the primary means of broadcast distribution.[101] The Committee made no acknowledgment of other demands for spectrum that might or should affect this policy, such as the need to accommodate growth in mobile services. In seeming reflection of this lack of priority, the telecommunications side of the British Post Office has only one person occupied with all forms of mobile radio—and this person also deals with other services, including cable television.[102]

There has been little discussion of personalized or mobile communications. The KtK report, for example, gave priority to the further development of conventional telephone service and treated mobile radio as a lesser form of point-to-point communications. It favored the deployment of radio paging, the beeper device that lets people know they are wanted on the telephone. This service conveys very little message information and makes minimal use of radio frequencies. Beyond that, the KtK called for standardization and intensification of "public land mobile radio," meaning such services as mobile telephone and the dispatching of taxis. It made no reference to the cellular system now being developed in the United States for these services, which requires considerable investment but which permits efficient re-use of frequencies within the same metropolitan area.[103]

The Annan Committee similarly proposed to squeeze mobile

communications to make room for expanded conventional broad-casting. "Despite the likely expansion of mobile radio services," it reported, "it seems to us desirable that additional frequency space should be made available for sound broadcasting, and this (VHF) band, or at least the lower half of it, would seem to be the most suitable for this purpose."[104] The Committee devoted no discussion whatever to the nature of the likely mobile demand or the social value or lack of value of mobile communications. The assumption seems to have been that everyone would recognize the superior claim on spectrum resources of oligopoly broadcasting. Yet it seems singular that this Committee—which would go to some lengths to draw a social distinction between the control of programming and the publishing of programs, and to push public policy in the direction of making room for the latter—could find no time or need to consider the relative merits of radio communication that is few-to-many (broadcasting) and radio communication that is many-to-many (mobile or personalized).

The Annan Committee did admit, on page 367 of its report, an allocation of frequencies for "private mobile radio." The concession was unexplained and it consisted of no more than half a Megahertz in the crowded radio broadcasting frequencies in the VHF band. For comparison, a single television channel in the United States uses six Megahertz of bandwidth; in Europe, where the picture is transmitted with 625 lines instead of 525, it requires more. The Committee did not consider the problems of interference by private mobile service with television and radio reception, which has been quite troublesome in America. Nor did it say anything about plans or pressures either to shift or expand the allocation of frequencies for "private" mobile use.

Citizens' Band radio, which has had so pronounced an impact on North America, has barely caught on in Western Europe. The CEPT, which is the association of European PTT's, has recommended orderly development of 12 radio channels for this service—a relatively meager allotment in comparison with the 40 channels set aside in the United States. A few governments, notably Germany, Sweden and the Netherlands, have accepted this proposal and are acting on it. Most have done nothing. In Britain, the Government has dug in its heels; the Prime Minister's office said in August 1977 that a CB service would intrude on other services and create serious problems of control.[105]

The disorderliness of Citizens' Band accounts for its guarded reception. Although it impacts on broadcasting, it falls under the control of the PTT, which as we have seen is dominated by engineering rationality. The PTT's systems approach and insistence on clear standards is offended by the disorganized patterns of CB use and by what is perceived as a wasteful use of scarce radio frequency resources. The social side receives almost no discussion (although there is now an effort by the British Post Office's Long Range Studies Division, which includes social scientists, to induce a reconsideration of present policy at senior levels in that organization). The result is, paradoxically, that radio frequencies are treated as a public resource so precious that the public cannot be allowed to participate in their use.

This European paternalism has apparently not been swayed by any effective manufacturers' lobby or by any upsurge of popular enthusiasm for personalized communications. The situation is different in Australia—admittedly a spacious country with larger communications distances to cover—where CB was recently legalized after it had flourished for more than a year with sets imported from the U.S. and Japan. Australia has now given its blessing, and 40 channels in the UHF band, to 50,000 previously illegal operators.[106] In the U.S., too, CB expanded dramatically after its use by truckers, who sought to evade lowered highway speed limits, entered the popular consciousness. Much of its appeal has been to the brash, rowdy and vulgar side of human nature. Perhaps in Western Europe, soccer matches already perform that function; there is in any case no political recognition of any unsatisfied demand that may exist for a more democratic use of radio communications.

2. *"Electronic Mail" and the Postal Service.*   The telephone, telegraph and telex have long substituted for letter mail and will continue to do so. On business matters such as financial transactions, however, which make up the bulk of first class mail, paper confirmation usually moves through the conventional mail system. Now, with such services as facsimile, computer conferencing, broadband cable and telephone text, there is the potential for supplanting letter mail entirely over a very large volume of traffic.

This raises a number of tricky economic questions: How should the new services be priced? Who should be permitted to offer them and on what terms? What sort of technical standardization should be imposed within and across national frontiers, and at what stage of service development? What effects can be anticipated on postal employment, and how might they be mitigated?

There are also a number of social issues to be addressed. These include the degree of privacy protection to be afforded electronic messages; the potential substitution of communities of interest for the geographic communities now sustained by physical mail deliveries; effects on spontaneity, felicity and even courtesy of expression if letter mail eventually dies out entirely—and the potential losses to history and biography in the same hypothetical case.

The economic questions, if not the social, are now being busily studied by the West European PTT's. The PTT's in the CEPT group have retained a private consulting firm in London to help think through the cost and service issues. In one major respect, these organizations have an apparent advantage: Since they hold a monopoly on both postal and telecommunications services, the losses they may face on one side can be offset by increased revenues on the other. Indeed, they can time the introduction of the new electronic services to coincide with the attrition rate of redundant postal employees.

But the situation is not quite that simple. For one thing, both computer-communication and telephone-text services can be offered by private entrepreneurs. To be sure, they will lease PTT telephone lines for the purpose. But since they will price their services to be competitive with postal rates, and will get a return for their own investment out of that price, the sums received by the PTT when supplying this service may not compensate for their losses on mail. Moreover, not all mail will go over to electronic delivery. For a long time to come, the postal routes will have to be served with a thinner mail bag but the same sets of legs. The quality of service almost inevitably will deteriorate, and the fall in postal revenues will not be matched by a commensurate drop in employment costs.

These matters are now being debated internally but there is very little public discussion and virtually nothing in the way of policy statements to guide public reactions. There was some consideration of the issues in both the KtK and Carter Committee reports, but for differing reasons they both seem inadequate.

The KtK conceded there is a problem. It found that 20 million out of 35 million letter items per day in West Germany are technically suitable for electronic transmission. Of these, six million are between businesses and therefore would be the first to shift over. Letter mail is already a deficit business, and it will most likely become necessary to slow down physical deliveries and to allow telecommunications to pick up the urgent messages. Yet the only recommendation made by the KtK was to carry out technical research into new terminals![107] That is not because its brief was narrowly technical. Elsewhere in its report the KtK identified values of self-realization and community that it thought telecommunications could serve, and in a broader sense it asked whether the information abundance ushered in by the newer technologies is not perhaps more than mankind needs.[108] Yet on the concrete and challenging issue of electronic mail, it passed up the opportunity to reflect on the implications for personal expression and social cohesion—let alone to resolve the complex economic and institutional questions presented by the new service.

The Carter Committee was not quite ready to accept that there is any problem. Its report consistently relegates the impact of future electronic message services to consideration in the future. For the present the "Postal Business" should hold firm:

> We have noted on our foreign visits pessimism on this matter, particularly in the United States. . . . Our judgment is . . . that though there may well be grave problems 20 years ahead, it is too soon to accept the decline of the posts as inevitable, or to embark on a descending spiral of service quality in a desperate attempt to hold off bankruptcy. The Postal Business should believe it possible to use its valuable monopoly to continue to provide a good service without subsidy.[109]

The Carter Committee understandably wanted no interference with its proposal to split apart the postal and telecommunications sides of the house. It did admit the existence of an argument that "there may be a need to develop a long-term communications strategy which recognizes that the Postal and Telecommunications Businesses are both engaged in the communication of messages." But it thought this could safely be treated as something separate from the issue of Post Office reorganization:

> We do not believe that the widespread adoption of new methods of message transmission which use *both* postal and telecommunications facilities is likely within a period that should affect present thought about organization; in other words, though there may be a shift of messages *across* the boundary between the Businesses, new developments which significantly blur the boundary are less likely.[110]

This line of reasoning seems somewhat difficult to square with the facts. First, boundary-blurring services already exist and are growing. In the United States, Mailgram service—a combination of telegraph long-distance transmission with local hand delivery by the postman—has proved very popular; and the U.S. Postal Service is now experimenting with intercity facsimile transmission. Second, the present and future shift of messages across the boundary is surely significant for postal policy as well as telecommunications policy: British Post Office projections quoted in the Carter report show telephone, telex, facsimile, mobile telephone, computer data transfer, radio paging and closed-circuit TV conferences as services that already can substitute wholly or partly for the mails. Viewdata telephone text and low-cost facsimile are among the new services—to which should be added "smart" typewriters—already in pilot or early operational stage. And the future is predicted to bring such wonders as "telemail," home delivery of newspapers, and color facsimile.

The prospect of such mail-diverting services may not undermine the validity of the Carter Committee's reorganization proposals; we have already seen that a consolidated PTT is not proof against economic disturbances from electronic mail. But the Committee's mandate extended also to assessment of "the policies, prospects and social significance of the Postal Business, including methods of financing it as a self-supporting public service." Looking at the financial issues in the United States, a Presidential Commission on Postal Service chaired by retired banker (and Aspen Institute Vice Chairman) Gaylord Freeman reported in 1977 that the situation offers only three choices: a further rise in postal rates, the curtailment of services, or the acceptance of huge public subsidies reaching some $12 billion annually by 1985. While these conclusions were not popular, they appear to be realistic and so to offer a solid foundation for policymaking.

The KtK and Carter Committee reports, it must be said, offer no such foundation. A wide range of economic, financial, technical and legal questions remain unaddressed in any public forum in Western Europe. Even more to be regretted is the stinting of questions of "social significance," on which the Europeans might have had much to offer to Americans. What about the post office as a center of community life, sometimes the center of its identity? What about the postman as a daily visitor to those shut in by illness or infirmity? What about letter writing as a social grace, even if personal correspondence makes up only a very small fraction of the whole mailstream? What, if anything, is it worth paying from the public purse for the positive values implied in those questions? And how can public policy be decided without asking them? Perhaps surprisingly, more overt attention has been given to these matters in America than in Western Europe.

3. *The effect on print of electronic innovations.*   If electronic mail has received little attention from policymakers, electronic publishing has probably received even less. Over the years, studies have examined the impact that television watching might have on the art and habit of reading, but no concerted focus has been brought to bear on the effect that the electronic information explosion in all its forms might have on the publication of books, magazines and newspapers.

Thus, the KtK ran its eye with general approval over the abundance of new services made possible by technological innovation: microelectronics, versatile terminal equipment, fiber optics, both broadcasting text and telephone text, facsimile, broadband cable with a return path for two-way communications, video discs and video cassettes.[111] It wondered whether all of the information made possible by these devices would be necessary: Is man prepared to become *homo informaticus?* But it thought that some of the new capacity, *e.g.,* two-way cable, could strengthen citizen participation in political activity. And it mentioned—without elaboration—the likelihood of an adverse impact on the print medium from electronic makeup and transmission of text information.

That impact could come from video discs, from cable systems connected to a computer or from teletext. Newspaper proprietors have tended to concentrate their concern on the third of these potential threats. They proposed to the Annan Committee a five-year moratorium on deployment of the British broadcast teletext systems—CEEFAX and ORACLE—for fear of losing both the revenue of classified advertisements and the readership attracted by stock market price listings. The Committee turned them down and promised only that there could be a review of the situation after several years of broadcast teletext operation.

The publishers fared no better with the Royal Commission on the Press, which did concede that the Viewdata type of telephone text system, with its very high information storage and dissemination capacity, would pose far more of a threat to their operations. The Committee refused to accede to the suggestion that newspa-

per publishers be allowed to protect themselves through a prescriptive right of participation in ownership and management of
the electronic medium. That same question is still being debated
in West Germany.[112] As we have seen, there is nothing in the nature of the telephone text service that would preclude full participation by publishers as information suppliers or even as competitive operators of the service. *The New York Times* already operates
a massive information bank of computer-retrievable articles from its
own files and from 60 other current affairs publications; access to
subscribers is through the telephone network, using a video display terminal and a keyboard in much the way that Viewdata
operates. The *Financial Times* of London announced in January
1978 its own entry into the marketing of electronic information services. More such activity is to be expected.[113]

But if and as newspapers "go electronic," will they stop conventional printing or raise hard-copy prices substantially? The fear that
newspaper availability might be curtailed has moved public policy
in Western Europe before. In the Netherlands, for example,
where bloc advertising is permitted on television through the
state-controlled STER monopoly, various proportions of the resulting revenue have been earmarked by the Government for payment
to the national and provincial press as compensation for lost newspaper advertising. (This arrangement, in force from 1967 to 1977,
has now been stopped.)[114] Similar thinking lay behind the Annan
Committee's foreshortening of revenue possibilities for its proposed fourth channel. And, of course, the desire to keep alive a
flourishing and pluralistic print press has nurtured the variety of
newspaper subsidy schemes in Western Europe that we examined
earlier. If the movement towards electronic text distribution inten-
sifies, and governments still wish to foster inexpensive paper distribution, the next Royal Commission on the Press may have to re-
consider present British aloofness to such subsidy schemes.

But this is only one of the possible dimensions of the problem.
Newspapers could conceivably do so well with electronic publishing that they themselves can subsidize the price of "hard-copy"
editions. Facsimile editions might eventually replace newsprint
with no damage to society at all. And yet it is those "social costs"
that need attention. What do we as a society stand to lose if conventional newspaper publishing, or the production of magazines or
books dries up? Will the quality publications go first or will they be
the ones to survive? Will electronic distribution attract govern-

ment controls over content, similar to those now imposed on broadcasting, and thus diminish the independence of the press? Or will the relative ease of access to the medium attract new publishers with a greater diversity of views? What social benefits, perhaps greater than those foregone, may be ushered in by electronic publication? On these quite basic issues, the policy dialogue in Western Europe has thus far been silent.

D.   The Convergence of Communications Modes

Traditionally, the telephone, the newspaper and television have been regarded as separate enterprises fulfilling different functions and subject to differing forms of governance. To be sure, there has been overlap: Both the telephone and the newspaper provide weather information; and where commercial broadcasting is permitted, it can compete with newspapers for advertising. But in the main, the nature of the messages conveyed, and the techniques for conveying them, have been seen as entirely dissimilar. Print culture offers portability, extensiveness, variety and ease of second reference. The telephone links individuals together and overcomes space and time constraints in both social and business transactions. Broadcasting captures a mass audience and offers real or apparent simultaneity of experience. It has been possible to view communications in rather neat compartments for purposes of policy formulation: print vs. electronics, one-to-one vs. one-to-many, distributed vs. switched message services.

Now all that is changing, although perceptions of, and responses to, the change are hesitant. The KtK recognized the emergence of what it called a "technical transmission integration." Fiber optics, for example, will be able to carry both narrowband (voice, data) and broadband (television signals) information. With teletext, similarly, the KtK could see a breakdown of the distinction between print and broadcasting. But the most the KtK was prepared to say about such developments is that they raise the urgent question of adequate future organizational structure— which is a political question.[115]

The Annan Committee flirted with this political question when it addressed, but did not resolve, the issue of integrating in a comprehensive fashion governmental competence to deal with communications policy. It considered the creation of a Ministry of Communications to merge executive responsibilities for broadcasting, aid to film and press industries, the arts and telecommunications. The Committee agreed that "the present separation is likely to cause problems when the technology of the services becomes indistinguishable and the borders between the services gradually become blurred." But it divided on whether to propose a consolidation of government functions, and ultimately retreated to the proposition that the allocation of responsibilities among ministries is a matter for the Prime Minister.[116]

The particular conclusion was probably sound. The idea of a Department of Communications has been considered informally in the United States for several years but has never been formally proposed because of doubts, first, that enough supervisory business could legitimately be accumulated to warrant creation of a new Cabinet department and, second, that such an entity would restrain its normal empire-building propensities sufficiently to stay clear of illegitimate activities such as censorship and the control of communications in the name of national defense. Yet the need to develop some sort of integrated capacity for dealing with complex and interrelated communications policy issues is readily accepted in the United States and was acted on by the Carter Administration during its first year in office. In Britain, the Annan Committee was most reticent with advice on this subject. The most it would venture is that "eventually governments will have to face the problem of communications policy."[117]

The Royal Commission on the Press did not face this issue at all. The Carter Committee did, but again in a cautious fashion. It admitted the possible need, as we have previously seen, for "a long-term communications strategy which recognizes that the Postal and Telecommunications businesses are both engaged in the communication of messages." But it saw no urgency about present development of such a policy:

> A long-term communications strategy is in any case a most appropriate subject for the Secretary of State's Council [on Post Office and Telecommunications Affairs] to examine; that is why we have proposed that there should be one Council, not two.[118]

This presumably will mean leaving such highly intricate questions as electronic funds transfers—with their impact on the mails, on banking (including postal banking) and on individual privacy—to an amateur body.

The Annan Committee displayed a similar penchant for deferral of the important policy issues presented by the convergence of communications modes. It devoted only two paragraphs out of a 490 page report (not to mention an Appendix volume of another 168 pages), to consideration of such issues.[119] Even so, this is more than can be found in other comparable West European documents.

The Annan Committee observed that broadcasting and point-to-point services are increasingly relying on common transmission techniques—microwave, cable, etc.—and over the next 20 years the two forms of communication will become less and less distinct. This blurring is likely to present a number of unspecified problems, some perhaps with far-reaching consequences. It will be necessary to define clearly the purpose of a service—why, it is not said.

In the future, the Committee thought, with broadband communications perhaps making use of optical fibers, the responsibility for transmission may have to be divorced from the responsibility for programs. (This is, of course, the position taken in 1974 by the then White House Office of Telecommunications Policy.) By the 1990s there may have to be "formidable changes in the consitutional arrangements for what are now called broadcasting services." *But not now:* The next 15 years, in the Committee's view, would provide an interlude between eras, from broadcasting as a separate service to "the era of multiplicity of telecommunications services." And so the policy issues can be postponed.

To appreciate what is at stake, it may be useful to offer a brief impressionistic recap of the source and nature of inter-service confusion. The distinction between print and electronics is being confounded by teletext of both kinds, computer teleprocessing and computer conferencing, the video disc, electronic funds transfer, and photocomposition. Mass media and point-to-point services are converging through cable, satellites, optical fibers, teletext and slow-scan video. Multi-capacity terminal equipment, capable of displaying video or audio or printout messages, will further combine previously divergent services. Technically, it may still be proper to distinguish between distributed and switched communications; but when the same apparatus can be used to deliver or display message services of either kind, the distinction may not be very significant.

What policy implications does this have? West European countries do not regulate their communications through a statutory commission; they have no need to recast a governing charter like the U.S. Communications Act of 1934. Still, as the Annan Committee put it, there are "constitutional arrangements" of both a legal and a customary sort, and structural traditions in industry and in government that will need review. To take just two specific examples, we may consider content controls and monopoly.

Over the next 15 years, audiences for traditional broadcasting fare will likely be fragmented appreciably by the use of television sets for teletext, TV games, video discs, television-computer links and the like. Political surveillance over programming, of the kind now practiced in Western Europe, is going to seem progressively less compelling and less effective. Long before it is renounced or abandoned, the case for common-carrier treatment of a medium that has acquired such versatility will begin to press for acceptance. That is, as the Annan Committee has put it, broadcasting authorities may come to be treated as publishers—and eventually neutral publishers of material presented for transmission. If the programming can get into the home in any case on an optical fiber tied to a computer, or on a video disc bought in a bookstore, why continue to insist on prior approval by broadcasting editors?

The abundance of choice of message services is likely also to force rethinking of monopoly communications structures. If the public can obtain what it wants from a variety of sources, then even if the government seeks to control all those sources, it will have great difficulty compressing them into a single organizational mold. More likely, it will abandon the effort at control and allow a certain diversity at least in the private market. The change will probably come haltingly rather than in one dramatic break; but for that reason, it seems all the more unlikely that policy planning can be safely deferred until the change takes place.

IV
Evaluation

Cultures may be more important than structures in explaining communications policymaking in Western Europe. Thus, in Sweden, the land that aspires to total freedom of information and the place where the ombudsman originated, a certain social timidity mingles with the desire for moral superiority. Only in this light can one understand the television "taboos" and the failure to use the full freedom Swedish broadcasting has in principle been granted. Similarly, the struggle to attain social parity among religious and class organizations in the Netherlands, the suspicions engendered by the Manichean political traditions of France and Italy, the party dominance and decentralizing impulse in postwar West Germany, the continuing reliance in Britain on "the right chaps" to sort things out—all these tendencies play a major role in determining how policy is decided.

Despite these important differences among the countries we have surveyed, there remain common trends or common points of distinction from the way that communications policy is made in North America. We may look first at the respective roles of the three branches of national governments—executive, legislative, judicial—in deciding policy, then consider how various advisory bodies do or could contribute to the process, and turn at last to a consideration of comparative value preferences: how West European policymaking looks from an American perspective, and how Europeans would judge American communications policy.

A. Government Policymaking

1. *The executive.*   The policy initiative and major power of control over European communications developments rests with the exec-

utive branch, or "the government" as it is called. Governments direct the PTT's, formulate the terms of broadcasting licenses and choose the managers. If changes are to be made or resisted, governments decide. This is very different from the situation in the United States, where broad powers have been delegated to an independent regulatory authority, the Federal Communications Commission, which is itself subject to the policy oversight of standing committees of Congress.

The absence of such a mechanism in Western Europe means that policy is arrived at largely behind closed doors, without the participation of all interested groups and without the public being advised what decisions are being considered. For example, the Long Range Studies Division of Post Office Telecommunications in Britain engages in periodic study of what it calls business policy issues. In early 1978, it was looking at the scope of the PTT monopoly and asking afresh who should be allowed to offer what services. Should there be a demonopolization of terminal equipment, or packet switching, or other old or new services? The established Post Office policy and the arguments on which it rests were being scrutinized, as were arguments on the other side. All the available evidence was being similarly assessed, for eventual presentation to senior officers.

No doubt the exercise will be highly valuable but it will have been conducted entirely in the dark. Supposing the Long Range Studies analysis is soundly conceived, there will be no assurance that any senior policymaker will be moved to adopt it. Supposing it is factually in error in some material respect, no knowledgeable outsider in industry or in a university or elsewhere will have a chance to correct it—unless the government should choose to set up a public inquiry committee, whose strengths and limitations we shall consider later. Predominantly, the process of executive decision-making in Western Europe is quiet, internal and publicly invisible.

No doubt it would be an uncertain and time-consuming process to introduce processes of public engagement into communications decision-making. The Australian experience is instructive.[120] Starting with a PTT structure derived from Western Europe, the National Telecommunications Planning Branch in Australia produced in early 1976 a report entitled *Telecom 2000*. One of its recommendations was to inaugurate a process of "open planning," and it followed its own proposal by distributing 20,000 copies of the report. Only 111 substantive responses were received, 41 of these from academics and students. Many were cynical about the prospects of opening up what they regarded as a rigid bureaucracy, and others emphasized the need for public education about telecommunications. The conclusion reached was that it might require 15 years to evolve a fully effective system of open planning, provided there were the political will to do so. In Western Europe, there has not as yet been any sustained intellectual curiosity, let alone political commitment about such matters.

Although much more government control over communications enterprises is exercised in Western Europe than in the United States, the consolidation or coordination of executive interests in communications policy has not been carried as far. There is nothing to compare with the former White House Office of Telecommunications Policy or the present Office of Assistant Secretary of Communications and Information in the Department of Commerce. Posts and telecommunications are consolidated in Western Europe but broadcasting falls under a separate ministry and neither can stake a confident claim to new technologies and services. On occasion this may produce a degree of useful competition: Development of the British Post Office's Viewdata system was probably accelerated by the introduction, not previously coordinated, of the BBC's CEEFAX and ITV's ORACLE. On other occasions, the contretemps yields simply a stalemate, as in the rivalry between the French PTT and TDF over the introduction of teletext.

No grand scheme is imposed from on top, which is probably all to the good. But there is also no coordinating mechanism to sort out competing claims or to establish priorities for the future. The Annan Committee, as we have seen, shied away from a Ministry of Communications and proposed no structural substitute for it—just as the Carter Committee declined to accept the logic of its own perception that the various modes of message delivery are all interrelated and becoming more so. The result is that executive policy formulation tends not only to be internal but also segmented and short-range in character.

2. *Parliaments.* In theory, West European legislatures could make up for this deficiency by establishing clear and purposive statutory mandates and by conducting public hearings to hold min-

istries accountable. In practice, this does not happen. The 1974 broadcasting "reforms" in France, for example, were pushed through the National Assembly in a matter of days and with no explanation of purpose. Since no performance objectives were stated, and none can be fairly implied, it is impossible to judge whether any significant improvements in the French broadcasting system have, in fact, been achieved.

The executive retains the important rights not only of appointment to key offices but also of acting by decree. This can carry a good deal farther than the American practice of exercising broadly delegated power through issuance of substantive regulations. In France brand advertising was introduced to television in 1968 by executive decree, even though the matter was then being debated in Parliament and the Conseil d'Etat was unwilling to say that it fell outside Parliament's jurisdiction. This power to issue decrees can also be used to frustrate the will of Parliament. In 1972, after passage of a bill granting a right of reply for broadcasting—a measure the French Government had opposed—the decrees spelling out the practical details of the right were withheld for more than a year and then the matter was passed to an advisory body for further consideration.[121]

The French Assembly has had its successes, for example in creating that independent advisory body—the Haut Conseil de l'Audiovisuel—and in giving it potentially important monitoring functions we shall examine later.[122] Like its counterparts in Western Europe, the French legislature also retains the right to approve or disapprove the level of broadcasting license fees. This gives it a significant veto power, and the French Parliament recently forced the reduction of an increase that was being sought. But this is a blunt weapon, not one crafted to deal with the nuances of communications policy. Although an annual report may accompany the license review, of necessity it is *ad hoc* and reactive in character.

Part of the difficulty experienced by West European legislatures arises from the structure or lack of structure of their committees. The relevant French committee is the Finance Committee, consisting of 61 members and responsible to oversee all government departments. It does not meet in subcommittees. One member takes responsibility for review of the RTF, and he is assisted by one highly knowledgeable and full-time staff adviser. The reports are literate and informative, but the committee members' schedules do not permit time to indulge in speculation about long-range or comprehensive policy.

Some members of the Annan Committee would have corrected this deficiency by creating in Britain a Standing Conference or Committee of Parliament on Broadcasting. They thought Parliament should have a mechanism for assessing the annual reports of the broadcasting authorities (the BBC and IBA) and for what Americans would call continuing oversight. The majority of the Annan Committee feared, however, that this arrangement would bring pressure to bear on the Home Secretary to intervene in the day-to-day conduct of broadcasting. On balance, the Committee decided, the existing chain of accountability between the government and Parliament and the broadcasting authorities was adequate.[123]

Proceedings of the European legislative committees are in any event not open to the public in the way that meetings of committees of the U.S. Congress are. In March 1978, one committee of the British Parliament caused a stir by opening its doors as a cautious experiment into what this would do to the conduct of witnesses and members. It may be a long while, if ever, before legislative hearings regularly supply the public visibility that is now missing from executive policy deliberations.

Another problem for legislators is the need to demystify complex and seemingly convoluted communications policy choices. This becomes apparent when one moves beyond the simple-seeming and relatively graspable world of broadcasting to the more intricate world of telecommunications and in particular the new technologies and services. West European legislators and party officials know that something significant is happening or could happen through the fusion of computers and telecommunications and satellites and fiber optics and multiple-capacity terminal equipment. But like the small sample of the Australian public responding to the *Telecom* 2000 report, they are not inclined to enter the policy dialogue until and unless they get a reliable education in the technical, economic and social aspects of what is going on.

This is a continuing need: Two years after the KtK report, a member of the executive committee of the West German Social Democratic Party appealed privately for such assistance, which he said should be useful to politicians of all parties throughout Western Europe and could not be drawn from civil servants or manufacturers or other vested interests. He recognized, as other legislators may not, that the foregoing of political decisions out of ignorance or uncertainty is itself a very important form of decision making, which will allow the future to be determined by happenstance or by lower-echelon executive judgments and not by reasoned political choice.

Of course, a broader reason for legislative incapacity relates to the general feebleness of West European parliaments vis-à-vis their executives. The system of ministerial responsibility, designed to assure that ministers and the executive would be accountable to their party majorities, seems almost to have been turned around so that today it is the members who owe loyalty to their ministers. Politicians talk increasingly of how this must be changed, and the all-party Select Committees in the British Parliament offer one example of how to assert a separate legislative judgment. But the exceptions seem still at this point to prove the rule.

At the root of the phenomenon there appears to be a growing ideological separation and suspicion between the dominant parties. Shared assumptions are declining in strength, separate assertions growing. No longer is this tendency confined to the Latin countries. The Conservative and Labor parties in Britain harbor increasingly strident doctrinal factions, which work against their respective needs to court support from the minority Liberal and Scottish Nationalist parties. Similarly in West Germany, the SPD and FDP on the left, and the CDU-CSU on the right, glare suspiciously at each other across the floor of the Bundestag.

In the Latin countries, the process has been carried to the point of forcing real or potential collaboration upon parties that have long proclaimed their antithetical roles. How can the Christian Democrats and the Communist Party of. Italy resolve upon a common policy for restructuring the RAI or for regulating the independent local broadcasters—including ideological broadcasters—admitted into operation by the court? How will decrees be formulated, and appointments made, in a France where the Communists and Socialists may have either a majority or near-majority in the Assembly while the Gaullists and Republicans continue to hold the Presidency? There is at present no ready answer to these questions.

3. *The courts.* Judicial forays into communications policy-making can perhaps be best understood in this setting of partisan distrust and stalemate. The West European courts, in general, are

not as likely as their American counterparts to get into the decision of basic structural issues. Again there is no independent regulatory agency with a statutory provision for systematic judicial review, nor are there the organized and litigious citizens' groups who are attracted into business by such an arrangement. So when the supreme tribunals of Italy and West Germany do make far-reaching pronouncements, it is an exceptional occasion meriting careful attention.

When West Germany's Federal Constitutional Court upheld in 1961 the constitutionality of the public television monopoly, it was arbitrating between the Länder and the Federal Government, between the Bundestag and the Chancellor, and to a perhaps lesser extent between the then dominant CDU (or more likely a portion of it) and the other parties. It rebuffed Chancellor Konrad Adenauer's attempt to introduce commercial television, thus performing the classical role of a constitutional court: deciding not what was the right policy but who was entitled to formulate that policy and whether its formulation was within acceptable tolerances—in this case, within the free-speech and federalism provisions of the German Basic Law.

The Italian Constitutional Court's decision of 1960, likewise upholding the constitutionality of the RAI monopoly, was similarly "legitimate" in the sense of American legal tradition. Its decisions of 1974 and 1976, however, were of a very different order. First, they asserted a judicial capacity to determine all the relevant facts and considerations without particular deference to the findings of the executive. Some of the factual determinations of the Court were, in fact, dubious: Imported broadcast signals may interfere with the use of domestic frequencies,[124] and even highly local broadcasting operations of the type the Court authorized may in the aggregate undermine the economic basis of the monopoly national service. These discrepancies highlight the essentially antidemocratic character of judicial decision-making, and the reasons in Anglo-American tradition for confining it to a secondary or reflective, rather than primary or initiating, role in policy formulation.

The same is also true of the Italian Court's dictation of a charter of rights and responsibilities for the RAI—a highly political act, substituting the Court's judgment in considerable detail for that of the Parliament and its contending parties. In traditional American practice such a judgment—going well beyond the facts or requirements of the case—might well be deemed an unconstitutional advisory opinion, entitled to have no force or effect.

But the matter emerges in a different light if one considers the immediate effect on the political process of issuing the court's charter. It could serve as a liberating document, relieving the partisan stalemate that for so many years had blocked any effective reform of the RAI. Certainly, the Communists and the Christian Democrats may have difficulty agreeing on implementing legislation. But RAI is the politician's television; it is the one medium that can give any of them nationwide exposure, can cover party affairs and party policy statements. No Italian politician of any party can simply stand by and watch RAI founder. Furthermore, in resolving disagreements over RAI legislation, all parties will have recourse to the same guidelines laid down by the court; and this too may expedite the task of reaching political accord. In this instance at least, an essentially antidemocratic judicial pronouncement may have served to liberate the political climate for democratic decision-making and indeed may have been indispensable to it.

One factor stimulating an activist judicial role, then, is the presence of a partisan stalemate or confrontation which tends to paralyze the democratic process of policymaking. That situation is also pending in France, where the parties of the left and the parties of the right have battled to a close parity. A further Parliamentary election is possible before the 1981 Presidential contest, and one way or another, the powers of the Presidency as against those of the Prime Minister may come to be tested in a manner not previously experienced under the Constitution of the Fifth Republic. The higher French courts that review the *Radio Fil Bleu* decision, setting aside the government monopoly over broadcast transmission, are likely to take that political context into account.

Those courts will also have to take account of the written guarantees of freedom of expression that exist in the Constitutions of Italy and West Germany as well as France.[125] The lower French court rested its decision expressly on such a clause, just as the Italian court formulated its RAI charter as a way of squaring the public broadcasting monopoly with the Constitutional assurance of free speech. In American constitutional history, free speech has evolved into the position of a "first freedom," claiming primacy over all other constitutional values. A similar evolution in Western

Europe could have far-reaching consequences for the structure and operation of broadcasting and of other electronic conduits for expression.

The French lower court also based its decision on the free-speech provisions of the European Convention on Human Rights.[126] In Britain this would make no immediate difference since that Convention is not incorporated into British law (and Britain, of course, has no written constitution or bill of rights). British practice could, however, ultimately be challenged in the European Court. In other nations signatory to the European Convention, its provisions typically have been incorporated into domestic law, so that the French judgment, if affirmed on appeal, could become an important precedent for the courts of such nations. The potential for judicial recasting of West European broadcasting policy is extensive.

To recapitulate the role of the West European judiciary, it appears that courts may intervene in communications policymaking if (1) there is a partisan stand-off impeding the operation of the democratic process and (2) fundamental social values are seen to be at stake. The first condition may be found in an advanced stage in France and Italy and to a lesser but still significant extent in most other West European countries. The second condition will be present when basic constitutional guarantees such as liberty of expression are involved. But there are other important values affected by communications policy—such as privacy, equality, fairness, economic opportunity—and these may or may not be recognized by participants in a lawsuit. Furthermore, planning for an uncertain future is something for which courts are by nature not well suited. We must consider how the policy planning process, and the identification of significant values, occurs in Western Europe outside the formal hierarchies of government.

B. Policy Advice

1. *Committees of inquiry.* The study committees whose reports we have been examining are likely to have exerted a measurable impact on communications policies in their countries. Some will have immediate effects on industry practice. Many of the Annan Committee recommendations, for example, were directed to the BBC and the IBA and can be implemented by them. Governments will

also respond and in some cases have already responded. The KtK's pilot projects for broadband cable have already been authorized by the competent West German officials. The Carter Committee's report appears to have stimulated the appointment of two senior people in the Post Office with a hospitable attitude towards the development of advanced telecommunications services. Specific further policy changes are expected over time, although the opposition of the major postal workers' union makes the splitting off of posts from telecommunications uncertain. A Government White Paper on the Annan Committee's report has already been issued and may result in legislative proposals before the next general election.

This record of political backing is better than can be ascribed to many presidentially-appointed or -approved study commissions in the United States. The Carnegie Commission on Public Broadcasting had the advance support of President Lyndon Johnson, and its report was swiftly translated into legislation setting up the Corporation for Public Broadcasting. But President Nixon dismissed the reports of studies into obscenity and drug abuse and emasculated others—such as one he himself had commissioned on oil import controls—very soon after receipt. In the United States, unlike Western Europe, study committees seem to be appointed as a way of deflecting controversy rather than resolving it. With the possible exception of the Royal Commission on the Press, the West European inquiries we have been examining appear to have been launched with a government commitment to some genuine follow-up action.

Yet that commitment seems not to extend to grappling with "future shock"—Alvin Toffler's expressive phrase for the tendency of future events to project themselves into the present. Particularly in electronic communications, where the development of technologies and services has been so rapid, there is a need for integrative and forward-looking policy planning. Unless the future of print and of the mails is analyzed now, they may be simply overwhelmed by new developments. Put differently, if policymakers wait until future developments become a present reality, the choices open to them will be much slimmer than they are today.

The West European committees of inquiry recognized these truths but did little to espouse them. The KtK remarked that the accelerated progress of technical telecommunications innovation

forces a focusing on "basic measures" to adapt to change.[127] But
the question of adequate future organizational structure, while
urgent, was a political question to be left to governments. The
chairman of the KtK, invited in April 1976 to speak to the annual
Telecommunications Policy Research Conference at Airlie House,
Virginia, declined to be drawn out on institutional changes that
might be necessary for West Germany. There may be current consideration of these matters; but if so, it is being conducted quietly
and not in response to proposals from the advisory committee.

The Carter Committee similarly was prepared to concede, at
least for the sake of argument, that old barriers are breaking down:
Postal and telecommunications enterprises "are both engaged in
the communication of messages." Although "a long term communications strategy" may be needed to deal with the implications
of this perception, it was not to come from the Committee. Instead, the task of developing such a strategy was to be given to an
independent Council. And even the establishment of that Council
was wrapped up in a recommendation to split the postal and telecommunications businesses—a proposal that faces an uncertain political future.

The Annan Committee perhaps went furthest in appreciating
the need to revise present structures for the conduct and governance of communications enterprises. In fact, in its view "formidable changes in [those] constitutional arrangements" might be
required to deal with the coming "era of multiplicity of telecommunications services." But the Committee thought consideration
of these changes could be safely deferred for 15 years, before which
time there presumably would be another committee of inquiry to
deal with the issues. The most poignant statement to be found in
any of the committee reports is the Annan Committee's confession
of its own inability to agree on how all the intersecting trends in
communications policy might be drawn together:

> But eventually Governments will have to face the problem of com-
> munications policy.[128]

The incapacity of the inquiry process to face this problem in all
its dimensions is difficult to explain. The committees took two or
three years to conduct their inquiries; they were open to submis-
sions of evidence, and they had ample opportunity to confer with
government officials and others. Some have suggested that the key

lies in the appointment of the committees' members. In Britain, it is said that the pool of candidates from which inquiry committees are drawn constitutes a kind of social club, whose members understand that their task is to engage in polite mutual self-criticism, nothing more. If a new idea departs uncomfortably from the *status quo*, it is unlikely to be carried very far.

This thesis, however, does not fit all the facts. There does exist a British Civil Service list of "the great and the good," as it is called; but the Annan Committee members, at least, were deliberately not drawn from it. Efforts were made, instead, to cull representative membership from among academics, blacks, women, television professionals, political party members, etc.[129] The KtK made an even more systematic effort. That committee was made up of: one designee from each of the four political parties, two representatives of the Länder, one from a local authority, two from industry, two from communications manufacturing, two from trade unions, two from broadcasting, one from publishing and one journalist. There were also five professionals—an electrical engineer, an economist, a communications scientist, a lawyer and a teacher of business administration.[130] Clearly, any failure to deal with the issues did not arise from the caliber or competence of such members.

Another possibility is that the committees lacked adequate expert counsel. The staffing of the Annan Committee was evidently weak in this respect, and briefing papers on technical developments were not made available. One Committee member, Professor Hilde Himmelweit, has stated that, in consequence, the Committee's chapter on "New Services and Technological Developments" is the weakest in its report.[131] Others say that a short-term inquiry with a predetermined agenda does not provide the amplitude for really informative testimony by academics and experts. To the extent that this is so, it could help explain the tentativeness with which the implications of new developments were treated in the inquiry committee reports.

But again, the membership of at least the KtK included all the professional disciplines and the industry experience needed to probe the technical, economic and legal issues. This was not simply a gathering of generalists, unable to deal with the mounting complexity of telecommunications developments. If even the KtK fell short in dealing with "future shock," the root explanation must lie elsewhere.

2. *Advisory councils.* The missing grasp could be supplied by the creation of continuous advisory bodies and this is apparently what the Annan Committee had in mind in some of its recommendations. It proposed that the mandate of an existing Television Advisory Committee, which serves the Home Secretary, be widened into that of a Telecommunications Advisory Council. Presumably, it could then deal with the whole multiplicity of expected services. Although its expertise would still be confined to one department of government—and would not extend directly to Post Office telecommunications or to print services—such a council could lay a solid technological foundation for a review of intermodal issues by the next committee of inquiry perhaps ten years from now.[132]

The Annan Committee also proposed the creation of a Public Enquiry Board for Broadcasting (PEBB), which might serve the useful function of making the public aware of the choices presented by new telecommunications systems and thus of preparing public opinion to give its informed consent when decisions have to be made. Curiously, the Committee proposed that every seven years the PEBB review how the broadcasting authorities have discharged their responsibilities. This looks like duplication of functions already performed by the authorities themselves, by the Home Secretary and by Parliament. In a time of retrenchment of government expenditure and consequent mistrust of new layers of government, the recommendation faces uncertain acceptance. (On comparable grounds, the Annan Committee itself declined to accept the suggestion of a Broadcasting Council as an independent "tribunal of taste"; that responsibility, it judged, should stay with the broadcasting authorities.) Yet the basic idea of holding policy hearings, as a vehicle for public participation in the assessment of policy options, seems sound. It could give an advisory body like the PEBB the confidence to propose far-reaching reforms, if warranted by the evidence and supported, or at least not opposed, by pressure groups or the public.[133]

It may be that the Annan Committee wanted to give the PEBB both specific and general obligations so that its political advisees would gain the habit of paying attention to its reports. The failure to devise such a credible mandate is one of the defects in the Carter Committee's proposal of an independent Council on Post Office and Telecommunications Affairs. Although the Council would be asked to look forward and devise "a long-term communications strategy," nothing in its proposed makeup or procedures would confer any particular legitimacy on its conclusions. It could easily become a means of deferring action rather than of taking it.

On the print-media side, press councils seem ill-suited for dealing with future communications policy. Press councils do not, as a rule, get into larger policy questions, such as the role of print media in the information delivery systems of tomorrow. They tend to act rather as defenders of what the press is doing today; and because of past press dominance of the councils, they have been viewed as something of a bastion for the *status quo*.

One recently constituted continuous advisory body may deserve closer examination. This is the Haut Conseil de l'Audiovisuel, created by the insistence of the French Parliament in 1972. It is composed of six members of Parliament, chosen by the Senate and the Chambre des Députés, and 34 other "highly qualified persons" from the arts, culture, science, technology, the law, professional and family associations and trade unions; these 34 are selected by the Government and receive three-year appointments, which may be renewed. At present, the Haut Conseil includes in its number some very distinguished and far-seeing people.

The Haut Conseil has no direct supervisory authority over the RTF, but it reports to the Government both on its specific statutory assignments and on other matters falling within its general competence. It prepares an annual report on the conformance of each of the broadcasting networks with its "cahiers des charges," or regulations. Subcommittees have also been at work on an ethical code of practice for broadcasting, on implementation of a broadcasting right of reply, and on other matters specifically given to it by law. The Haut Conseil has no compulsory powers and so far has not held public hearings, but it has mediated among parties involved in the subject of its inquiries and its reports apparently are given more than cursory attention in the Government and Parliament.

Whether the Haut Conseil might go further and engage in persuasive future-policy consideration is not yet known. Its name suggests that it could advise the authorities on the whole direction and development of audio-visual technology, including interactions among different modes of information distribution. Nothing seems to prevent it from holding public hearings. But this would require a certain boldness of direction and independence of spirit which the French Government would presumably allow only if it attached a high priority to the work of the Haut Conseil. The moment for that, by all available indications, has not yet arrived.

3. *Independent agencies.* Interestingly, some observers have seen the creation or proposal of these permanent advisory committees as a step towards the setting up of West European regulatory agencies with a general jurisdiction, more or less on the North American model. The PEBB's policy hearings would follow the example set by the CRTC in Canada, although the PEBB would have no power to adopt or enforce regulations. Some of the Haut Conseil's members expect it to evolve in the direction of an FCC with mandatory powers; at present, the Secretary General (who happens to be President Giscard d'Estaing's son-in-law) believes that more can be done without such powers, through quiet persuasion and mediation. Even the Carter Committee's proposed Council on Post Office and Telecommunications Affairs is viewed by some as a potential forerunner of an independent regulatory agency, although the Carter Committee left the Council's mandate and composition too fuzzy to support any confident expectations.

These assessments of potential evolution are made by communications policy analysts who sense a need to develop the capacity for forward-looking and comprehensive planning. By and large, that sense is not shared by the European politicians who would have to authorize any new regulatory arrangement. In 1971, the Social Democratic Party in West Germany did adopt a resolution favoring establishment of a Federal Commission for Communications. To be created through interstate agreement (like the ZDF network), it would have been given only research, advisory and public information functions; even so, it has never come into being.[134] There is evidently a fear that any such body would usurp or encroach upon political responsibilities now within the province of governments and parliaments. Even more, there is lack of recognition that anything important will be lost if the West European planning process fails to encompass foreseeable communications policy risks and opportunities on a comprehensive scale.

4. *Political support.* Deficiencies in the scope of advisory inquiries are attributable, in the end, to irresolution of political will and imagination. It was not Lord Annan who decided there should be three entirely separate committees on the press, on posts and telecommunications and on broadcasting. It was the British Govern-

ment that failed to see the vital and growing interconnections among all these enterprises of message distribution. It was the German Government that similarly limited the writ of the KtK. The other West European governments failed to examine these questions at all. It is a point not of criticism but of praise that the inquiry committees did at least identify the broader questions and lay the foundations for future policy analysis on a wider scale.

Whether that challenge will be taken up by governments is by no means certain. In a time of recession and unemployment, are the new technological marvels anything more than conveniences or creature comforts? What priority can expanded or faster means of discourse legitimately claim in the national economy? And perhaps most important, who should decide those questions and with what set of social values in mind? It is because there is a significant difference between the American and West European perspectives on this last question that we close our report by considering it.

C.   Governing Values

The dominant fact about communications policymaking in Western Europe is its paternalistic character. A very small number of people—in governments, in senior positions in government-controlled monopolies, and occasionally in government-appointed advisory committees—reach almost all the relevant decisions. These people, who all know each other, tend to place the highest value on orderliness and stability and on what they judge to be quality. Standards of engineering elegance and cultural merit shape the concept of quality, and those standards again are applied by a small elite. If such arrangements slow the pace of service innovation or leave consumer tastes unsatisfied, the system is evidently willing to pay that price. Priority is in any case not given to attainment of economic efficiency or to the freedom of choice that might come with a more open system.

This can be seen in the treatment of capital investment requirements for new services. Both the Annan Committee and the KtK advised against the development of nationwide broadband cable systems on the ground of their very large capital costs. This may well have been a sound warning in the light of telephone text and video disc systems that will shortly be able to supply a full range of audio-visual information and entertainment services at much lower cost. But investment theory—or at least the theory prevailing in the United States—would leave that determination to the discipline of the private capital markets. If an entrepreneur fails to raise the needed capital, well and good; if he does raise it and then loses it because consumers prefer a competing service, this is seen as the best assurance that the right choice has been made. Market forces, in brief, are considered a better determinant of consumer satisfaction and also a better spur to service innovation than decision by a cloistered group of government officials.

This theory is plainly not accepted in current West European communications policymaking. Neither the Annan Committee nor the KtK even considered letting the pace of cable development be determined by private entrepreneurs. They would have seen such a decision as unreasonable. Rationalization and integration of communications systems are more to be prized than market competition.

Partly, this is a function of the constraints on both government budgets and on private capital in the wake of international oil price rises and the consequent protective measures governments in Western Europe have taken to contain inflation and unemployment. Partly, it is the reflection of a general preference for stability and order. The British Post Office, for example, is a major employer of low-skilled labor. It pays comparatively good wages and offers attractive pension and other benefits. This makes for a reluctance to risk upsetting the *status quo*, as could happen if electronic alternatives to mail service were allowed full freedom to develop.

But to a large extent, what is being resisted is private enterprise pure and simple. William Rees-Mogg, editor of the London *Times,* has asserted that public enterprises of the sort that run Post Office Telecommunications and the BBC exhibit far lower productivity than their privately owned counterparts in the electronic communications industry.[135] Adam Smith's *Wealth of Nations,* he reminded his readers, took as its first principle the improvement of labor productivity—a lesson that nations in economic difficulty should presumably wish to heed. But efficiency considerations have not been paramount in British or West European structuring of their electronic communications services, and there is no indication that this will change.

In the telecommunications field generally, the emphasis is on engineering standardization and the interconnectibility of systems.

Computers were developed first and standardized later, hence the high rate of innovation in that industry. But when a telecommunications user in one location has to be able to reach other users in a variety of other locations, standardization must precede development. That is the engineering ethos. As new technologies and services either fall within or must make connecting arrangements with the PTT monopolies, the primacy of engineering considerations within the PTT's makes for a widening application of this perspective—again, counter to that of market competition.

On the broadcasting side, the dominant considerations are social and cultural, not economic. Viewership is important in those countries like France and Britain and the Netherlands that have permitted programming rivalry to develop. But it has been introduced to make broadcasting more lively and informative, while leashing the tendency of audience competition to cater to the lowest common denominator of tastes. It is because the Netherlands' purposively open system has slipped into permitting entry to purposeless programming groups that its government is now, belatedly, considering tightened entry. The BBC's harmonization arrangements, and French broadcasting's quality index, further indicate a strictly limited indulgence for broadcast competition. The important programming choices issue from an "establishment" view of what is good cultural fare, as determined by the governors and directors of European broadcasting. For the main object of the enterprise is to offer up the nation's culture to present and succeeding generations. The market, with its taint of commerce, is at best a necessary interference.

All this could change, in the name of free speech, if the Italian precedent remains in force and spreads. Other West European countries could find themselves obliged to allow competitive entry at least into local broadcasting, as Sweden has already done. The French attack on the state transmission monopoly could carry even further. But none of these decisions is predicated on commercial or economic grounds, and the governments have not been the ones to take the initiative. So far as their policies are concerned, the system is an elitist one and should remain so.

Few West Europeans find any reason to deplore this state of affairs. There is none of the hunger for activism or participation in policy decisions that one associates with American citizens' groups. There is, of course, no forum like the Federal Communications

Commission to attract their petitions and other filings, and parliamentary committees do not engage in searching out dissenting or minority views in the public at large. The absence of public participation in policymaking allows the ministries and authorities and directors of communications enterprises to develop their options in private. They give themselves no chance to build political support for a policy departure that a Cabinet minister may find risky. It is a quiet business, to be decided by a handful of people who are presumed to know what is in the public's best interest.

From an American point of view, then, the West European process of communications policymaking would be faulted on at least two grounds: lack of public accountability and inattention to economic efficiency. But that is transporting values from one side of the Atlantic to judge performance on the other. The calculus can easily and instructively be turned around.

The West European attitude recoils from the squandering of finite resources, whether natural or human. If one communications system will do a particular job, it would be seen as senselessly duplicative to compete against it for consumer approval with another system. This applies in the procedural realm as well. An insistence on letting everyone have his say consumes a great deal of time and resources. In America, there is judged to be an overelaborate stress on procedural regularity, and altogether too much litigation. The reams of paper filed with the Federal Communications Commission—the emblems of public and industry participation—are too often wasteful and unproductive. If one is persuaded, as the Western Europeans are, that only a tiny number of people is qualified to judge the issues anyway, then all this fuss over participation simply confuses matters and delays or distorts a sound decision.

The capitalist system of entrepreneurial incentives is seen as having a proper place in building national character; but, in the communications field, this system must be kept in check because of its inherent tendency to generate waste and incompatibility. The proper role of government is to protect against the private abuse of monopoly powers. There is here a strong ideological notion that the essential infrastructure for information distribution in a society should be kept under the control of the State, together with a political equation of the State with the government of the time.[136] The people's interests, their liberties of thought and expression need safeguarding; but governments and their public-service motives are more to be trusted for this purpose than the interplay of businesses and their profit motives.

If this seems dangerously Orwellian to many Americans, the failure of America to take the same approach looks insensitive to West Europeans. Even among well-traveled Europeans who do not hew to the "establishment" line in their own countries, America as a communicating society tends to be viewed as remarkable but not admirable. Personal enrichment and not enlightenment is seen as the *summum bonum*. Greed is glorified, taste and discernment are not. That is how the American commercial broadcasting system is judged, as the give-away of an enormously important social asset to people who fritter it away to make money satisfying the baser human wants.

These European critics have heard the American counterarguments and they are not impressed. Certainly, the West European system is paternalistic; but it is a paternalism built on the conviction—itself born of experience—that what people want is not necessarily what is good for them. Wisdom and quality are the key ingredients, and they are not supplied by market forces or public participation. If one offers a light entertainment program on public or commercial television, its aim should be to capture an audience for the quality program that follows—just like Shakespeare after limericks in a classroom.

The Europeans recognize what they are excluding. In the unregulated sphere of popular music, it is the American-style songs that dominate in every capital and that link young people on both sides of the ocean in a kind of folk-culture Esperanto. This is tolerated, but not any farther than it has to be. Where communications are subject to government control, measures to limit this leveling influence are taken in order to preserve the higher forms of national culture.

Americans tend to say that the market must be relied on because no government can presume to decide what is in the best interests of the variegated public. But Europeans rejoin that they have pinned their faith on the possibility of getting a better wisdom than that of the marketplace. This is more than just a 17th century disdain for commerce, although that enters into the equation. It is a positive emphasis on quality in an artistic sense; and if it is patronizing, then so were the Medicis.

On this basis, the Europeans would fault American broadcasting for the low quality of its programs, although they do not hesitate to use those programs as golden bait for the audiences they want to lure towards quality. They would find the American emphasis on competition and innovation to be exaggerated and often wasteful. And they would see little merit in a paper chase conducted on behalf of some ideal of public participation rather than of sound decisions.

It would be agreeable to find some way of melding the best aspects of the two systems. Quality, wisdom, innovation and public engagement should not have to be mutually exclusive. But the emphasis given these various characteristics on each side of the Atlantic is the product of divergent social philosophies. The role of governments in particular, and the confidence reposed in them, are very different. In Europe, a continuing class system permits and even encourages policy decisions to be taken by the few on behalf of the many. Curiously enough, social democracy in its root sense is far stronger in America than it is in Europe, and it would not allow governments to control the power of choice as widely as has happened in Western Europe. American reliance on market forces is based on a populist distrust of governments, just as European reliance on government control is anchored in a concern to protect the cultural patrimony from business exploitation. There is not much room for reconciling these opposing social perspectives.

The West European approach to the planning and use of communications systems might be said, historically, to have produced certain advantages. Decisions could be reached with a minimum of procedural delay, and they could be based on shared perceptions of wisdom and quality—two values whose importance can scarcely be denigrated. In the stable and relatively simple world of point-to-point communications, broadcasting and the press, this process of policymaking worked well. The telephone network might not operate as well as the American (it still does not), but the mails were probably better and the quality of newspapers and magazines and radio and television programming was very often superb.

In the past ten years, however, the tranquility of these European arrangements has been disrupted by a series of technical advances collectively dubbed "the information explosion." No longer are communications enterprises fitted into three simple compartments; instead, many service configurations interrelate with and converge on each other. The process of policy decision has become much more complex, so that it is doubtful any government can harmonize the multiplicity of choices. It seems that market development and competition will have to be allowed substantial roles in the sorting out of service arrangements, and the American policy-making process is more attuned than the West European to dealing with this state of affairs. Furthermore, if Europeans today grumble that they are being pushed by Americans towards the new world of communications diversity and abundance, it may be in part because their own system has not been sufficiently open to allow their own societies to do the pushing.

The communications policy challenge now facing both America and Europe is sufficiently novel and far-reaching to preclude any smugness on either side of the ocean about the adequacy of established institutions or processes. Creativity of a high order will be needed to recognize and manage the upsetting complexities of the future. As both Old World and New begin composing themselves to accept this new responsibility, each may in time discover that the values and traditions of the other are less alien to the task than had at first appeared.

Footnotes

Some of the sources cited here are the papers and remarks presented at two conferences held at the Aspen Institute in Berlin. The first, sponsored by the Aspen Institute's Project on Communications Policymaking, was convened in March 1977; it is referred to as "Aspen Berlin Conference I." The second, sponsored by the Writers and Scholars Educational Trust, was held in January 1978; it is cited as "Aspen Berlin Conference II." The papers at this second conference are being edited by the authors under the supervision of Anthony Smith for publication during 1979 under the tentative title *Politics in Camera: Television in the Political Life of Western Europe*.

A full listing of the participants in the two Berlin conferences may be found in the Appendix.

1 *Report of the Commission for the Development of the Communications System*, Federal Ministry of Posts and Telecommunications, Bonn 1976.

2 *Report of the Committee on the Future of Broadcasting*, Cmnd 6735, HMSO, London 1977.

3 *Report of the Post Office Review Committee*, Cmnd 6850, HMSO, London 1977.

4 *Report of the Royal Commission on the Press*, Cmnd 6810, HMSO, London 1977.

5 Carter Committee report, para. 8.1(a).

6 See Alfred Grosser, *Television in Politics: The Federal Republic of Germany* (draft paper presented at Aspen Berlin Conference II); remarks of Klaus von Bismarck and Herman Wigbold at that conference.

7 Annan Committee report, paras. 4.14–.25.

8 See, *e.g.*, Antoine de Tarlé, *La Télévision et la Société Politique Française* (draft paper presented at Aspen Berlin Conference II); cf. interview with Michael Tyler, managing director of Communications Studies and Planning, Ltd., London, March 1978.

9 Mahle and Richter, Communications Policies in the Federal Republic of Germany 78 (UNESCO, 1974).

10 van der Haak and Spicer, Broadcasting in the Netherlands 29 (International Institute of Communications—Routledge and Kegan Paul, 1977). The struggle over introduction of any advertising on Dutch television was bitter and prolonged and was instrumental in the downfall of the government in 1965; the present system was inaugurated in 1967. *Id.*, at 19–20.

11 Annan Committee report, para. 15.25.

12 See de Tarlé, *supra* note 8; Smith, The Shadow in the Cave: The Broadcaster, the Audience, and the State, 96–98 (Quartet Books, 1976).

13 See, for this entire discussion, de Tarlé, "Financing French TV/Radio," *Intermedia*, October 1977, pp. 29–32.

101

14 Commission des Finances de l'Assemblé Nationale, *Rapport sur la Radiodiffusion et Télévision Française* (October 1977), pp. 16-17.

15 *Télé 7 Jours*, Jan. 28–Feb. 3, 1978, pp. 20-21.

16 Rapport de la Commission des Finances, *supra* note 14, pp. 14-15, 18-20, 25-28.

17 *Télé 7 Jours*, Jan. 28–Feb. 3, 1978, pp. 108-111. There is also a centrally administered "harmonization" system in the Netherlands, but it is used simply to avoid duplicative buying of identical programs. The process works like the registration of mining claims and likewise offers arbitration. van der Haak and Spicer, *op. cit. supra* note 10, pp. 47-48.

18 The structure was, in fact, imposed by the Occupying Powers, who confiscated the Third Reich's radio transmitters and later turned them over to the authority of the Länder. This arrangement was confirmed in the German Basic Law, or constitution, before the Allies relinquished their reserve powers over German broadcasting. See Mahle and Richter, *op. cit. supra* note 9, p. 17.

19 See *id.*, at 23, for a description of the history and of the interested parties—prominently including Chancellor Adenauer—involved in the litigation. See also Grosser, *supra* note 6, p. 4.

20 See *Télé 7 Jours* for the FR3 regional programming schedule; Jan-Otto Modig, *Recent and Proposed Changes in Broadcasting Structures* (paper presented at the IIC Annual Meeting, Washington, D.C., September 1977); Annan Committee report, para. 7.10.

21 See Modig, *supra* note 20, Appendix. The discussion in this section is based largely on Åke Ortmark, *Boundaries of Freedom in Swedish Television* (draft paper presented at Aspen Berlin Conference II) and on remarks by Ortmark at that conference.

22 Ortmark, *supra* note 21, p. 3.

23 *Id.*, at 40, 50, 54-56.

24 *Id.*, at 17-18.

25 Much of the ensuing discussion is drawn from Herman Wigbold, *The Government's Role in the Dutch Broadcasting System* (draft paper presented at Aspen

Berlin Conference II) and from Wigbold's remarks at that conference.

26 Up to ten percent of broadcast transmission time, and the use of NOS studios and personnel, is also made available to churches, spiritual societies and political groups that serve cultural or social needs not otherwise being met. van der Haak and Spicer, *op. cit. supra* note 10, p. 24.

27 The emergence of competition for viewing "numbers" among Dutch programming organizations has drawn attention to the distortions produced by counting supporters on the basis of magazine subscriptions. A poll taken in 1975 showed that fully 55 percent of all members subscribed because of the attraction or reputation of the magazine, while only 30 percent were drawn by their political or religious beliefs, and fewer than 15 percent rested their decision on the quality of the radio or television programs. TROS owes much of its success to production of the cheapest program guide, which is marketed through the business side of the largest national newspaper. The other groups have engaged in vigorous self-advertising on television for their own magazines. If membership were divorced from subscription to a program guide, it has been calculated that the affiliation share of the largest organization, AVRO, would be reduced by half whereas VPRO's membership share would more than triple. To date, however, the Dutch authorities have been unable to agree on an alternative measure for the size of support constituencies. van der Haak and Spicer, *op. cit. supra* note 10, pp. 64-66.

28 This account of developments in Italian broadcasting is based largely on Fabio Luca Cavazza, *A Country and Its Style: Television and Politics in Italy, 1954-1977* (draft paper presented at Aspen Berlin Conference II), and on remarks by Furio Colombo at Aspen Berlin Conference I.

29 Judgments No. 225-227, Italian Constitutional Court, July 10, 1974.

30 Cavazza, *supra* note 28, p. 1.

31 *Intermedia*, December 1977, p. 8.

32 Cavazza, *supra* note 28, p. 1. The Italian government has recently shut down the retransmission stations carrying Swiss

and Yugoslav broadcasts, claiming interference with aeronautical and military operations, but the validity of this action has not yet been tested in court. *Intermedia*, December 1977, p. 7.

33 *Intermedia*, February 1978, p. 2. The decision has more recently been affirmed on appeal, but the possibility remains of a further review by the Cour de Cassation.

34 This is not to suggest that the European press is everywhere unfettered in its journalistic coverage of events. Laws of libel and contempt are often more restrictive than in the United States. Britain's Official Secrets Act shelters far more information about government activities than anything sanctioned in American law, and indeed the U.S. Senate expressly rejected comparable provisions contained in the recently proposed recodification of the federal criminal laws. There are also security restrictions on certain kinds of reporting, such as those imposed through the British "D-Notice" system. But none of these asserts a systematic right of review or control of press content by ministers or other instrumentalities of government, as takes place with broadcasting.

35 Royal Commission report, pp. 61, 113. See generally Smith, Subsidies and the Press in Europe (PEP, 1977). For a short summary of measures adopted in the various Nordic countries, see Furhoff, Jonsson and Nilsson, Communication Policies in Sweden (UNESCO, 1974).

36 The Dutch Minister of Culture did propose in 1974 that financially ailing newspapers be aided by specific subsidies conditioned on their journalists' being allowed to participate in editorial decisions. While the aim seems benevolent and perhaps even progressive, the principle would entail interference in press autonomy; perhaps for this reason, the proposal has not been adopted. See van der Haak and Spicer, *op. cit. supra*, p. 88.

37 See Royal Commission report, pp. 196 ff.

38 *Id.*, at 4.

39 *Id.*, at 41–42.

40 See Smith, Telecommunications and the Press (British Post Office, 1977).

41 See Royal Commission report, p. 32.

42 "Germany Divided Over Cable, Teletext," *Intermedia*, October 1977, p. 4.

43 *E.g.*, Royal Commission report, pp. 148–149.

44 Interview with Alex Reid, Viewdata project manager, Cambridge, February 1978.

45 Henri Pigeat, "New Electronic Communications Systems: The French Example," *Issues in Communications*, No. 1 (International Institute of Communications, 1977), p. 43.

46 See KtK report, pp. 167–170; *Intermedia*, October 1977, p. 4.

47 Pigeat, *supra* note 45, p. 44.

48 KtK report, p. 143.

49 Pigeat, *supra* note 45, pp. 43–44.

50 See "A Chart of Teletext Systems," *Intermedia*, February 1978, p. 12.

51 KtK report, p. 147.

52 "How the Post Office Wants to Use Viewdata," *Intermedia*, February 1978, p. 13.

53 See the KtK report, p. 45.

54 *Id.*, at 54.

55 Interview with Dr. James Cowie, Long Range Studies Division, British Post Office Telecommunications, Cambridge, February 1978.

56 Remarks of Herman Wigbold at Aspen Berlin Conference II.

57 van der Haak and Spicer, *op. cit. supra* note 10, pp. 70–71.

58 Peter M. Lewis, "The Italian Experience: Lessons for Others," *Intermedia*, October 1977, p. 19.

59 Annan Committee report, para. 15.21.

60 *Id.*, paras. 9.5, 9.7.

61 *Id.*, paras, 15.23, 15.25.

62 *Id.*, para. 15.30.

63 *Id.*, para. 3.2.

64 *Id.*, para. 3.14.

65 *Id.*, para. 14.50.

66 See *id.*, para. 3.13.

67 See van der Haak and Spicer, *supra* note 10, pp. 12, 91.

68 *Intermedia*, December 1977, p. 3.

69 KtK report, p. 161; cf. Annan Committee report para. 25.20.

70 KtK report, p. 175; see Annan Committee report, Ch. 25.

71 KtK report, p. 75; cf. Annan Committee report, Ch. 25.

72 Smith, *op. cit. supra* note 12, p. 276.

73 Annan Committee report, paras 3.23, 8.49.
74 Interview with Alan Sapper, head of ACTT, London, November 1977.
75 Interview with Dr. Heinz Rathsack, director of the Deutsche Film und Fernschakademie, Berlin, January 1978.
76 Remarks of Dietrich Schwarzkopf at Aspen Berlin Conference II.
77 Anthony Smith, *Passive but Impartial; Television and Politics in Britain* (draft paper presented at Aspen Berlin Conference II), pp. 30–31.
78 Ortmark, *supra* note 21, p. 13.
79 *Id.*, p. 49.
80 Remarks of Klaus von Bismarck at Aspen Berlin Conference II.
81 Smith, *supra* note 77, p. 24.
82 Ortmark, *supra* note 21, p. 12.
83 Wigbold, *supra* note 25, pp. 31–33.
84 The French have proposed a monthly televised summary of Parliamentary activities, edited so as to show portions of principal debates and oral exchanges, which could be very interesting but seems likely to offer a programming rather than a legislative event. Haut Conseil de l'Audiovisuel, *Rapport sur la Mise en Oeuvre et le Respect des Cahiers des Charges des Sociétés de Radio et de Télévision* 13–14 (1977).
85 Smith, *supra* note 77, pp. 26–29.
86 van der Haak and Spicer, *op. cit. supra* note 10, pp. 2–3, 35.
87 Smith, *supra* note 77, pp. 24–25.
88 *Id.*, at 22.
89 Annan Committee report, para. 16.45.
90 van der Haak and Spicer, *supra* note 10, p. 28.
91 Annan Committee report, para. 6.17.
92 These clauses are cited, and the basis for the following discussion, may be found in Smith, *supra* note 77, pp. 21–22, 31–33.
93 de Tarlé, *supra* note 8, pp. 29–34.
94 See Grosser, *supra* note 6, pp. 7–9.
95 Remarks of Klaus von Bismarck and Dietrich Schwarzkopf at Aspen Berlin Conference II.
96 van der Haak and Spicer, *supra* note 10, pp. 23, 30.
97 *Id.*, at 35, 70.
98 *Id.*, at 27, 43.
99 Annan Committee report, para. 15.18.

100 *Id.*, para. 15.20.
101 *Id.*, para. 14.34.
102 Interview with Dr. James Cowie, Long Range Studies Division, British Post Office Telecommunications, Cambridge, February 1978.
103 See KtK report, pp. 105–107.
104 Annan Committee report, para. 25.6.
105 *Intermedia*, December 1977, p. 2.
106 *Ibid.*
107 KtK report, pp. 128 ff.
108 *Id.*, at 74, 88–89, 91.
109 Carter Committee report, para. 10.49.
110 *Id.*, para. 9.8 (emphasis in original).
111 KtK report, pp. 68–72.
112 *Ibid.*
113 See Rex Winsbury, "Newspapers' Tactics for Teletext," *Intermedia*, February 1978, pp. 10–11.
114 van der Haak and Spicer, *supra* note 10, p. 39.
115 KtK report, pp. 69–72.
116 Annan Committee report, paras. 5.30–.32.
117 *Id.*, para. 5.31.
118 Carter Committee report, para. 9.8.
119 Annan Committee report, paras. 25.1, 25.2.
120 Frank Wion, *Current Work on Telecommunications Policies and Structures* (paper presented at the IIC Annual Meeting, Washington, D.C., September 1977).
121 See Thomas, Broadcasting and Democracy in France, 98–99 (Bradford University Press 1976).
122 *Id.*, at 99–102.
123 Annan Committee report, para. 5.38.
124 Cavazza, *supra* note 28, p. 25.
125 *E.g.*, Italy: "All are entitled freely to express their thoughts by word of mouth, in writing, and by all other means of communication" (Article 21); Federal Republic of Germany: "Everyone shall have the right freely to express and disseminate his opinion by speech, writing and pictures and freely to inform himself from generally accessible sources." (Article 5.)
126 Patterned closely after the Universal Declaration of Human Rights, Article 10 of the European Convention guarantees "freedom to hold opinions and to receive and impart information and

ideas without interference by public authority and regardless of frontiers."

127 KtK report, p. 68.

128 Annan Committee report, para. 5.31.

129 Interview with Lord Harris of Greenwich, minister responsible for broadcasting in the Home Office, London, March 1978.

130 KtK report, pp. 18–21.

131 Interview with Hilde Himmelweit, Annan Committee member, London, November 1977.

132 Annan Committee report, ch. 6.

133 *Id.*, paras. 6.30, 16.47.

134 Mahle and Richter, *op. cit. supra* note 9, pp. 54, 57.

135 William Rees-Mogg, "Shares for Workers; Freedom for Managers; Profit for Britain," London *Times*, February 6, 1978, p. 12.

136 See, *e.g.*, de Tarlé, *supra* note 8, p. 30. President Giscard d'Estaing has declared that henceforth the State should be no more than an instrument of service to the people, *id.* at 36, but to date there has been no relaxation of government control over either the PTT or the RTF.

Appendix

POLICYMAKING FOR OUR COMMUNICATIONS FUTURE

Aspen Berlin Conference I
March 16–19, 1977

List of Participants

Lord Annan
  Provost
  University College
  London

Michel Audoux
  Telecommunications Division
  Commission of the European
    Communities
  Brussels

Douglass Cater
  President, Observer International, Inc.
  Director, Program Council, Aspen
    Institute for Humanistic Studies
  London

Furio Colombo
  La Stampa
  Rome

Jean D'Arcy
  Chairman
  International Institute of
    Communications
  Paris

Henning Dunkelmann
  Institute for Urban Studies
  Berlin

Hans Peter Gassmann
  Head, Informatics Studies Unit
  OECD
  Paris

Hilde Himmelweit
  London School of Economics and
    Political Science

Roland S. Homet, Jr.
  Program Director
  Aspen Institute for Humanistic Studies
  Program on Communications and
    Society
  Washington, D.C.

John Howkins
  International Institute of
    Communications
  London

Manfred Jenke
  Director
  Westdeutscher Rundfunk
  Köln

Edgar Kull
  Axel Springer Verlag
  Berlin

Marc Porat
  Fellow
  Aspen Institute for Humanistic Studies
  Program on Communications and
    Society
  Washington, D.C.

Glen O. Robinson
  Special Adviser, Aspen Institute
  Professor, University of Virginia, School
    of Law
  Charlottesville, Virginia

Murray Seeger
  Los Angeles Times
  Bonn

Uwe Thomas
  Ministry for Research and Technology
  Bonn
Michael Tyler
  Post Office Telecommunications
  Cambridge
Jean Voge
  Président du Conseil de
    Perfectionnement
  De L'École National Supérieure des
    Télécommunications
  Paris
J. S. Whyte
  Senior Director
  Post Office Telecommunications
  London
Eberhard Witte
  University of Munich
  Institute for Organization
  Munich

Aspen Institute Berlin
Aspen Institute for Humanistic Studies

TELEVISION IN THE POLITICAL LIFE OF WESTERN EUROPE

Aspen Berlin Conference II
January 15–17, 1978

List of Participants

Klaus von Bismarck
President
Goethe Institute
Munich

Roger Errera
Judge
Conseil d'Etat
Paris

Alfred Grosser
Professor d'Etudes Politiques
Paris

Wolfgang Haus
Director
Institute for Urban Studies
Berlin

Roland Homet
Aspen Institute
Program on Communications and
Society
London

Gerd Kopper
SPD-Executive Committee
Bonn

Lothar Loewe
TV Commentator
Norddeutscher Rundfunk
Berlin

Robert McKenzie
Professor of Sociology
London School of Economics and
Political Science

Åke Ortmark
TV Commentator
Stockholm

Michael Scammell
Director
Writers and Scholars Educational Trust
London

Dietrich Schwarzkopf
Deputy General Manger
Norddeutscher Rundfunk
Hamburg

Anthony Smith
Research Fellow
St. Anthony's College
Oxford

Antoine de Tarlé
Broadcasting Consultant
Comité des Finances
Assemblé Nationale
Paris

Herman Wigbold
Newspaper Editor and Broadcasting
Commentator
Netherlands